THE RIO

TAPE / SLIDE ARCHIVE

Contents

Previous pages
The Tape/Slide Newsreel Group outside the Rio, October 1983. Big films that month included *Olivia* by Jacqueline Audry, Merchant Ivory's *Heat and Dust*, and Rainer Werner Fassbinder's queer masterpiece *Querelle*. There were also nine days of live music concerts, and a call to the community to participate in a tape/slide project called 'One Day in Hackney' (see pp 78–85) – 'a unique picture of Hackney life as we, the people of Hackney, see it. Anyone can take part!'

Foreword
Michael Rosen

I lived in Hackney from 1978 until 2011 and long before that I was a regular visitor to Sandringham Road, where my grandparents lived. As a result I have a view of Hackney as a constantly changing, evolving place. The part of Hackney where my grandparents lived was mostly Jewish, while the parts of Hackney that I lived in later were a mix of people with origins in places all over the world alongside people who had lived in and around London's East End for several generations. But it wasn't only the people who were changing; the buildings and streets were too.

In the period covered by this book, I was living in Homerton and then Dalston. I had a strong sense that underneath the name Hackney there were 'villages', each with their own identities. Chatsworth Road was very different from Ridley Road; Homerton High Street very different from Kingsland Road. I loved the way that simply by walking down a street, or shopping, or visiting schools – as I often did – I could get a sense of new and old communities trying to make the best and the most from the circumstances. I could also see that for some – perhaps many – life wasn't particularly easy. It was a struggle to make ends meet.

In this context I remember taking part in various campaigns, particularly around education and anti-racist action in relation to deaths in police custody. My first two children were in Hackney primary schools at this time, and issues around Hackney's difficulties in retaining staff had a direct effect on what I could see going on with my children. Looking back, I have one or two regrets that we weren't able to create a more united front of parents, children, school students and teachers. One campaign where

Above and above opposite
1983: the Hasbudaks had come to the UK from Turkey but their two children, Zeynep (8) and Fatih (6), were born here. When their parents were selected for deportation, parents and staff at William Patten School campaigned to reverse the decision. Michael Rosen (opposite, far left) is dressed as Dr Smarty Pants from the Channel 4 kids TV show *Everybody Here* at the request of the pupils

Left
Zeynep Hasbudak (second left) and her schoolfriends

Both photos from the 'Hasbudak Deportation' newsreel, April 1984

it was possible, though, was the anti-deportation campaign organised at William Patten School. A gross and unfair intervention by the government was directed at deporting two Turkish parents of children who had been born in England. We did all we could – I think, in the end, unsuccessfully – to overturn the decision. At the time it did indeed bring together parents, children, teachers and the wider community. I can't help but think that this was in its own way a taste of things to come: the 'hostile environment' directed at migrant families, and of course the cruelty and tragedy faced by the Windrush generation.

Though I'm not still living in Hackney, I wish Hackney and the Rio in particular very best wishes and hope for the future.

Michael Rosen
Summer 2020

Foreword
Zawe Ashton

Opposite
A Save Hackney
demonstration passes
the Rio in 1984

When people ask me where I'm from, before anything else my soul answers: Hackney. I am a rich mix. My lineage is varied and vast. But the place that holds all of it is Hackney. Not even London! Hackney.

When I look through the photographs in this archive, I remember why. I see the Hackney of my babyhood, my childhood. I see images that evoke the lively sights, sounds and smells that would have been shaping me even before I had the language to describe what they were. The references to understand. Hackney hasn't just been a collection of postcodes to grow up in, it's been a way of life. I'm sure the rest of you who were there in its heyday, can testify to the feeling that Hackney isn't so much a place as a vibration. One that still resounds deep inside of me. The Hackney I see depicted in these fabulous photos – the Hackney of the 1980s and 1990s – is a world away from the Hackney we know now.

My Hackney was multi-generational, multi-ethnic. It was its own country, it seemed, its own planet. There were so many faces and voices that made up our community. As recently as the 1800s, Hackney was a village. That makes total sense. In lots of ways, it felt like a special settlement of like-minded people. A tribe. It would always surprise me when, outside the settlement boundaries, I would say with pride where I was from and be met with the most palpable discomfort. Judgment. Pity, even. 'Why?' I thought.

My tribe, was on the whole, an accepting one. A vivid one. We never judged anyone else, so why were we scorned? We were a tribe that protested where we saw injustice, organised, marched, made noise, were deeply concerned with equality. We put on raucous street parties, danced to music from across the world, provided funfairs,

puppet shows and affordable plays and community classes for children and adults alike. We created safe spaces for asylum seekers, survivors of abuse, the homeless. We demanded equal rights for women, mothers, carers, our queer community, the disabled, out of work, homeless, disenfranchised. We demanded reform when young black men and women were taken too early by criminally excessive force at the hands of the police. We called out racism for what it was. We protected our libraries, our health workers, our reservoirs, our schools, our cinemas, recreation centres, our independent businesses, independent artists, our burgeoning politicians.

There didn't seem to be an inch of Hackney that didn't hum with activity, creativity and revolution. Even the bus drivers seemed radical. I don't remember a conductor on any of the routes through Hackney that didn't wear their uniform with swagger, their conductor's caps every so slightly askew. An air of rebellion and of style, an energy informing the uniform. Informing us, the passenger, that their stories were more than the parts we saw. There was personality, a life behind the service (p 133). That seemed to be

everywhere. The sense that the local butcher had a story to tell. Our history was palpable and it gelled us all together.

Squatters, Beatty Road

There are so many photos in this archive that have stopped me dead in my tracks, transported me back to a precious time, a long-gone era of the borough I love. A time when Hackney really was all about community. The photos of pensioners and policemen trying to jump-start an ice cream van in the local park (p 123), the young interracial friendship groups collecting conkers (p 139) and riding the Ferris wheel at the summer fair (p 50), the older men and women with broad smiles in the bingo halls (p 214), the church halls and the protest marches. Gentrification has washed so many of these images away. I am lucky to have them seared into my brain and on my heart.

One of my favourite archive pictures is of two squatters sitting on a doorstep in Beatty Road. Not too far away, two of my neighbours had the same Day-Glo hair, bovver boots, torn clothes and punk attitude. For people outside our tribe, they were to be steered clear of, to arrest on sight, perhaps. Inside the tribe, they were our artists, musicians, friends and my sometime babysitters!

Another couple of photos that strike a chord are the Save Hackney tea party outside the Town Hall (p 52) and the Funk The

Wedding: Rock Against Racism festival in Clissold Park (p 40). Both these events were before my time, but they capture the essence of what I knew of Hackney in my early years. It was a place where culture, community and anarchy seemed to exist in perfect harmony. All art seemed politicised and vital. The photo of John Cooper Clarke performing onstage at a cooperative-run festival on Bradbury Street (p 66) strikes a chord. If you had a message to spread through poetry or prose, there was usually a stage for you!

Which brings me to the Rio Cinema, one of the most influential hubs of E8. Its roots are deeply political and there has always been a tussle over the space and that tussle has been about keeping it as a community resource rather than a tool for big business. It sits in the heart of Dalston at the apex of many schools and older people's facilities and served them brilliantly with special screenings. The Rio I've always known and the cinema I visited as a child for the playcentre and weekend matinees was welcoming, if not always physically warm! We took our own blankets back then, as the heating couldn't quite be relied upon, and there was a resident cat (p 103) who would come and warm your ankles if you were lucky. It was always somewhere I felt I belonged. Everyone was made to feel like it was for them – an accessible arthouse cinema that welcomed anyone in through its doors, whether it be to watch a film or to shelter from the cold with a cup of tea. It was at the Rio, days shy of my eighteenth birthday after handing in a brand new CV, that I got my first job that wasn't acting. I wanted to earn some money before drama school and working at this venue that held so many childhood memories seemed like a 'full circle' moment. I couldn't believe my luck when I was given the job. I learned how to usher, sell tickets, make proper coffee: I lived my American high school indie movie dream. Above all, I got to watch some of the most influential arthouse films of recent years, at least twenty times (and blockbusters too – there's a mother and baby screening of *Godzilla* that still haunts my dreams). They were joyful days, sitting in the heart of the community and remembering the Hackney that shaped me. However, it was through those same Art Deco windows that I saw that Hackney I knew start to fade. Older customers got older, passed on; young families grew and moved on. Over my seven years working there, I saw a younger, more affluent, community start to move in. The original settlers started to disperse. It's a tale as old as time and communities must change and develop rather than stagnate. But, as the High Street morphed from chemists, Turkish and Indian restaurants, hardware shops and greengrocers into more self-conscious bars and coffee shops, shops selling ironic trinkets that I couldn't imagine the original settlers having much use for... the Hackney of my childhood seemed to move further and further out of view.

These photographs feel so important, because they give an amazing insight into what came before. 'Before Hackney had the aitch!' as a cabby once said to me. (There are those of us who remember when black cabs wouldn't drive here, stopping on the outskirts of the City instead of heading towards the 'front line', as the borders of our borough were once dubbed.) They capture the tribe in a magic era of change and, in my memory, togetherness. They are a beautiful way for the old school to remember what was, and for the new school to understand the pulses and rhythms that underlie the material change. The radical energy of Hackney will resound in this book, as in the photo albums of all who were there at the time. The village spirit lingers on. I invite the new settlers to make caring for the community a conscious effort. The last bastions – like me – are here to keep the memories alive. As is this book. To celebrate the residents who are still safeguarding all we fought for, back in the day. When we were effortlessly cool. Unashamed. Vanguards of so many revolutions. No matter how tiny. We were all in it together. Please, if you love Hackney, enjoy this trip down memory lane. It still takes a village to keep justice, equality and peace at the heart of our communities. Hackney for life.

Zawe Ashton
Summer 2020

Shooting pool

Contributor biographies

For those people whose words are borrowed from other sources – Benjamin Zephaniah, CLR James, Mackenzie Frank, Julia Bard, Jag Patel – please see 'Acknowledgments and thanks' (p 254).

Barbara Schulz has lived in Hackney all her life, and in the same co-op since the age of 19 or 20. Joining the Centerprise and Rio groups gave her the confidence to go to university to train as a teacher.

BB (who wishes to remain anonymous) joined the Rio group after moving into a shared co-op house in Hackney in 1984. She was 23, unemployed and had just come out to her family and friends.

Carole Jasilek worked at a young people's advice centre in Leicester. She went to London for some time out, but returned and continued in community work.

Cat Thomas was originally from Gwent but Hackney has been her home since the early 1980s, when she threw herself into supporting the miners' strike.

Clovis Julien was a vehicle mechanic for BT Fleet, and led adult education classes in the evenings. He worked for Hackney Adult Education until 2019.

Colin St Leger was the teacher-in-charge of Hackney Downs's Unemployed School Leavers' Project from 1982-88. He worked with the RTSNG in 1987 and later at the Hackney Sixth Form Centre.

Dee Phillips was interested in photography and journalism when she joined the RTSNG. She later studied for a degree in Audiovisual Studies.

Eveline Marius had poetry published with Sheba Press and Centerprise. At the time of the RTSNG she was involved in youth work and mental health projects, and qualified in social work in 1986.

Felicity Harvest joined the Rio in 1982 after a career in the arts, community arts and the environment. She later became a Hackney councillor, worked for the Arts Council and is now a humanist celebrant.

Fern Presant lived in Hackney for thirty years from 1984. She worked with HAEI facilitating reminiscence groups and produced a sound newspaper for the visually impaired.

Guy Farrar worked at Centerprise in various roles, including developing the Young Photographers Group, and was part of Big Flame. He's since worked in community development and education.

John Paish was chief technician at the Rio from 1980 until 1985, introducing a new projection system and Dolby Stereo sound during his time there.

Katherine Hornak was a squatter and a long-time Hackney resident. She gained many skills while fixing up the places she lived and is still renovating old properties.

Keith Braid was living in his mum's house on Clapton Park with his wife Lorraine, both unemployed. They were both born and brought up in Hackney. He went on to work at the Rio and in community finance.

Maureen Carroll trained as a teacher in Ireland. She went on to a degree in Audiovisual Studies and when back in Ireland made radio documentaries.

Neil Martinson grew up in Hackney, was active in community politics and also a photographer. He splits his time between

Snowdonia and London and is working on another project about Hackney.

Ngoma Bishop was known mainly for promoting or supporting small community-based, arts-focused events, and as a performance poet. Before getting involved in Roach Family Support Committee he had no political affiliations.

Ramsay Cameron shared Rio programming duties with Robert Rider between 1982 and 1988. He then left on a year's sabbatical and had the opportunity to move into film-making.

Rebecca Brueton grew up on Greenwood Road, E8. Her politically engaged parents were the catalyst for her lifelong interest in politics, most recently, in feminist and environmental activism.

Sandra Hooper returned to London in 1981 after a course in Creative Photography in the Peak District, and worked in community arts projects. After nearly twenty years, she moved to Brighton and trained in therapeutic storytelling.

Thembi Mutch was studying at the LSE, and part of a wide community of squatters in Ellingfort Road. She worked part time at the Hackney Empire and as a girls' youth worker, and weekend nights at a residential care home.

Will Kemp previously worked with the Advisory Service for Squatters and HUMS. After the RTSNG he worked in community radio around the globe.

THE RIO SLIDE NEWSREEL PROJECT

This is the city. In the city there are many stories, a and the Rio is one of these. The Rio slide newsreel group will hope to cover many of the stories in Hackney that have an effect on, or involve, the local community. Our coverage will include hard news, ie. that covered by other media, but will also include local festivals, local events, and projects that we feel need to be high-lighted. As a group of 13 young people, many unemployed, we hope with the involvement of the community to bring alternative news to the general public. Funded initially by the Jubilee Trusts, with tutor hours from the Adult Education Institute, the slide newsreel group has been in existance since October, and will eventually bring a reg-ular newsreel to the cinema. This is the Rio. This is one of its many stories.

Left
The RTSNG's founding manifesto in the Rio's annual report for 1982

Opposite
The RTSNG archive as it was discovered in 2016

How we made this book / about the text

Tamara Stoll, Alan Denney and Andrew Woodyatt first met Sandra Hooper, Rio Tape/Slide Newsreel Group (RTSNG) leader, in 2017. In March 2020, with Max Leonard, a local writer and publisher, and designer Myfanwy Vernon-Hunt, we started making this book. First, that meant finding the original Tape/Slide Newsreel Group members and initiators, Rio staff and people shown in the photographs. We mainly conducted interviews via Zoom during the Covid-19 lockdown, with some via email or (socially distanced) in person. Once lockdown eased, we invited some of the members to view the slides on the new screen in the Rio basement, where they used to meet.

Edited, approved transcripts were then layered to create a virtual 'conversation'.

We made the photo selection according to the RTSNG's newsreel notes, and also chose shots to represent the Rio, the Tape/Slide Newsreel Group and Hackney life in the 1980s. Unfortunately, aside from a full VHS of 'One Day in Hackney', no original tapes or audio have been found.

We have linked images to newsreels and dates where possible: some refer to the event, some to when the newsreel was shown. Often slides would be reused in later newsreels, as background. We have had to leave many undated.

We are planning a new tape/slide newsreel workshop for young people in Hackney in 2021, working with some of the original members to recreate 'One Day in Hackney' forty years on, again to be screened at the Rio. The Rio Cinema is donating the photos to the Hackney Archives, where they will be freely accessible by the public. Alan is cataloguing the scanned images so the collection is searchable by people, places and events. The RTSNG archive will be an important resource for future researchers.

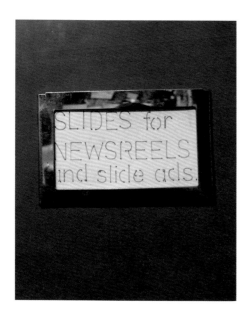

HACKNEY

Beginnings

NEWS

ROUND UP

The Rio and the Tape/Slide Newsreel Group

In 1979 the Rio became London's first community-run cinema. The management spent the next years working out what this should mean. Around 1982, that led to the creation of the Tape/Slide Newsreel Group.

Felicity Harvest (Rio coordinator): The Rio called itself a community cinema, and there were various kinds of programming, but to begin with what was on the screen was mainstream, apart from the Sunday afternoon 'arthouse' slot. So, at first, it wasn't seen like Centerprise or [other community organisations]. But once that perspective changed, it had something really important to say. The newsreel group got the Rio enmeshed properly into its community, it helped give the place credibility.

Ramsay Cameron (film programmer): I don't think the politics of that period can be understated as a determining factor in how we developed either the programme or the cinema itself. Thatcherism, unemployment, a growing consciousness around racism, increasing cultural diversity, AIDS, gender issues, the miners' strike, etc... But in contrast to that there was the Greater London Council (GLC) and Hackney Council, which still had budgets that allowed for the support of places like the Rio – and lots of others – and for generally progressive causes. If you look through the programmes, I think they show that we were responding to the political climate but also trying to be positive and inclusive.

John Paish (projectionist): Initially, my experiences at the Rio were not good.

During my first show, Dennis Crowley, the then manager and film programmer, burst into the projection room demanding I stop the film, as a customer was threatening to jump off the balcony. A few days later, being asked to sort out a plumbing fault in the Gents (projectionists were Jacks-of-all-Trades in those days), I discovered a cistern full of used hypodermic needles. ... Many customers would remind us that the Rio used to be a Tatler [see p 98], and I think its past was a real hindrance to early development as a community cinema. But I worked with some wonderful people while at the Rio. We had a common purpose and, although we always seemed to be dealing with problems, it was a pleasure to go to work each day.

FH: It was politically an exciting but frustrating time... Apart from the odd Ken Loach film, the vast majority of the medium of cinema presented a straightforwardly capitalist perspective, with often very dubious values in terms of women in particular. Our whole effort with the Tape/Slide group was to put an alternative view on the screen... It was all about putting a working-class perspective – often a black perspective, often a woman's perspective – on the screen. That was the *raison d'être*. Well, officially the *raison d'être* was raising the skills of young people, which I hope it did. That was the official reason – and that was a very good reason – but it went much further than that.

The Rio's resplendent candy stripes were the result of an architectural competition that went over budget; as a result, the box-office canopy was a bare metal skeleton for over a year. In the photo below, the Rio is hosting the British premiere of *Düşman* (The Enemy), a political thriller by Turkish director Yilmaz Güney, in November 1982

The Rio Tape/Slide Newsreel Group

Around the beginning of 1983, the RTSNG started producing material.

Sandra Hooper (RTSNG leader): Annette Giles was the instigator – she was the person from Hackney Adult Education Institute (HAEI), as it was known then, who approached me at Centerprise with a view to creating this new project at the Rio. It came out of the Young Photographers group and Hackney Unemployed Media Scheme (HUMS) at Centerprise. Community involvement was the whole essence of Centerprise and the Rio was very much a community cinema, so I suspect we came up with the idea of the newsreel as a way of bringing the community into the cinema, in a way that was actually pretty radical.

RC: We were collaborative, but we didn't participate much in the actual production of the newsreel or in the running of the project... From my own point of view I was very keen to reinvent the idea of the Pathé newsreels that used to accompany film screenings. In the early 1980s video technology was still expensive and 16mm too impractical and expensive, but tape/slide offered the possibility of doing something that could easily be projected onto the main screen, was cheap and could be produced quickly, and could be responsive to what was going on around us.

SH: It was a two-hour class, so we would meet for the first half hour and people would say what they were doing, where they were going, and they'd collect the kit they needed and off they'd go... it was a very fluid collection of people all with a single mission, which was to get something up on the screen.

Barbara Schulz (original RTSNG member): I started doing the Young Photographers and then I became part of HUMS, the youth unemployment group, making a magazine. Many of us from that group joined Sandra at the Rio and became part of the newsreel group, doing news, taking photos, deciding on what stories we wanted to cover. We used many of the skills we'd learned on the magazine.

We made decisions collectively about what issues we wanted to cover. Usually you'd go out in pairs, someone to take pictures, someone to take notes. If it was a demonstration, we'd probably go in a group, with a few of us with cameras, so then we could collate our stories and talk about what happened...

Everyone would go off and do their own thing and then we'd come back and decide together on which slides – because we just snapped away bang, bang, bang, you didn't know what you were going to get.

SH: I was facilitating rather than directing it, because the whole point of it was that it was a community newsreel. It wasn't a semi-professional or professional record, it was a comment from the inside. That's what made it special...

We represented quite a range of experience. I was very aware that I was coming in as a white, middle-class thirty-year-old, working with a huge variety of local young people, with very different experiences of life and futures ahead of them. What they had to say was very important. It wasn't being said anywhere else.

Will Kemp (original RTSNG member):
I think we had to more or less train ourselves – and each other, of course. We pretty much worked it out as we went along. Sandra had more ideas about some things and she passed that on to the rest of the group. I remember we used a basic form of what I later learned was called 'dub editing'. We made the soundtracks by copying bits of interviews from one tape recorder to another, connected via a cable, and built up the story that way.

BS: I don't think there was any training. I think we just learned on the go.

We were always looking at slides, choosing slides, putting them on the lightbox, mounting them, marking which ones we wanted, and then deciding who'd do the script, who had the best voice at the time. We'd put it together, then synchronise the images with voiceover, adding music and effects where necessary..

As we went along, different people acquired different skills. People were comfortable doing different things: some people liked asking questions; some people liked taking photos; some people enjoyed writing and putting it together. Not everyone attended regularly, you could pop in and out. I think I was there quite a lot of the time.

BB (later RTSNG member): I remember the first time going down into the basement and just thinking, this place is about to fall apart. I mean, the stairs down, they should have been condemned!

Keith Braid (later RTSNG member):
It was damp and quite smelly in our section, because I think the basement had only been opened up in the couple of years before it, and it was gradually being redeveloped. Other areas of the basement were being made into a mini cinema and a meeting space, but the bit we were confined to was the dampest by far. There was no natural light and it was pretty grim down there. But it was a space, and there was never that many people in the group at any one time.

BS: When we first started work down there, it was a dive, it was just like a scrappy, dirty... I think they used it to store boxes of popcorn and all the odd stuff for upstairs... There used to be lots of pipes across the ceiling and we used to mess about and do pull-ups on them.

BB: At the time I never really wanted to be a photographer. That wasn't my ambition. I always wanted to be a journalist, even when I was young. But I went to a really duff school and when I went to see the school's career person, she looked at me as if I was mad and said, 'Why don't you just become a secretary?' For me, the journalism was why I joined the group. I felt it was about learning a little bit of how to tell other people's stories. I was as interested in the interviews as I was in the pictures.

I didn't know one end of a camera from another when I started and I certainly didn't know how to interview anybody on a tape recorder. That was part of the learning of the group, all the technical side.

You felt it had a real sense of purpose.

WK: I seemed to be always going from place to place to do things, mostly around

Above
Members of the Tape/Slide
Newsreel Group and friends
on Kingsland High Street

Right and previous page
The group in the 'newsroom'
in the Rio basement, and out
on the job

the Hackney area. I remember a fair bit of time spent in the pub, drinking beer and playing pool – usually with Barbara and a few other friends – often at lunchtime after working on the newsreel or *Starting Out* magazine. In those days, pubs were closed during the afternoons, with slightly different opening hours on opposite sides of Kingsland High Street/Stoke Newington Road, and I remember we would sometimes cross the road to get an extra half-hour's drinking time before the afternoon closure. I think the Hackney side closed (and reopened) half an hour before the Islington side. Apart from that (and possibly because of that), it's all a bit hazy.

Dee Phillips (later RTSNG member): It was like an adventure, that's how I see the Rio newsreel group. There was always something new, and there were really supportive adults who would lead you and direct you and encourage you – and, yeah, let you be equal and have an equal say.

BB: We wanted always to tell the stories of people that we felt weren't being represented anywhere else at the time. There were only four TV stations, there was no such thing as social media... there obviously were national newspapers, but there were loads of stories that never made it to air anywhere. And so we set about finding them, telling them, and we felt like we were giving people a voice. Everyone could come along and see that they were being fairly represented and that we had told their story in an honourable way. That was the other thing that we were trying to make sure – that the stories we told a) weren't being told, but also b) they weren't being misrepresented either.

SH: When you go out and you take photographs and you talk to people you are no longer an observer: you're in it, rather than observing it.

BB: We only had the camera when we were supposed to be on a job, we weren't allowed to keep them. And everybody fancied themselves, like, 'I take really nice photos'... Everyone wanted to take really nice shots, obviously – you'd try to make sure that you'd got something in there that felt very beautiful, if you had that opportunity. Yes it was collective, but there was a little bit of competition between people. Then there was also just the honour of being able to meet people, talk to them and interview them.

JP: I recall Sandra and her team coming into the projection room with each new edition, to set up and programme the changes, having already prepared the soundtrack. I loved their enthusiasm and dedication, and I think we provided a unique opportunity for developing their talents and their interest in local affairs. I always looked forward to a new edition.

More importantly, the newsreels covered items that either escaped or were totally neglected by the local press and media, and became an important part of how the Rio was beginning to be seen by the local community.

BS: The newsreel group was good because you felt you owned it: you had a say, so it was *yours*. It wasn't like the BBC News or the old Pathé newsreels.

Vans parked outside the Four
Aces club on Dalston Lane

Below
The Gibbons department
store on Amhurst Road sold
furniture and toys. It burned
down in 2003

Above
Queuing to sign on at
the Spurstowe Terrace
dole office

Left
Jobless figures displayed
on Hackney Town Hall, 1983

Opposite
The JobCentre on the
Narrow Way, Hackney Central

Hackney in the early 1980s

When the RTSNG first met, Margaret Thatcher was surfing a wave of success in the polls after the Falklands War, on her way to a second term in office. But the combination of decades of neglect and Conservative policies were hitting Hackney hard.

Eveline Marius (poet, youth and mental health worker, RTSNG collaborator):
It was a very discontented era, with people disillusioned, frustrated, angry. There was high unemployment, bad housing. Hackney was seen as one of the disadvantaged boroughs. There was a lot of discontentment, people just felt like there was nothing happening. And a lot of groups rise up after the 1981 riots. There was a lot of demonstrations. At the time they called it Poll Tax, now it's known as Council Tax, demanding money from people who have no money. A lot of people were homeless.

KB: I grew up in the 1960s, and there were big changes in terms of immigration into the borough by the 1980s but the fundamentals didn't really change. It was always a place of, sounds corny, but a place of struggle and violence. They were always there around the corner, and you always had to be aware of that, just in case something kicked off or, you know, you got approached by someone you didn't want to be dealing with.

BS: Unemployment was high, housing, job cuts, the miners' strike, Thatcher – no one liked her, so we were all united in the same arguments, on the same fronts. All us young people didn't have anywhere to live, we lived in squats, we lived in short-life housing, which is what I did.

Most of us, we'd got our UB40 and we'd meet down Arcola Street or down Spurstowe Terrace and sign on. So we were all in the same boat.

BB: We all knew that we were not part of the big project – and we were never going to be part of the big project – and it felt like we were never going to have any money. All of the other side of it that you see from that time – you know, people in the City making loads of money – that was just like another world we saw on TV but didn't really know anything about.

Everybody I knew was on the dole. At least there was a dole then! I don't even think there is a proper dole now.

Thembi Mutch (later RTSNG member): Income support was meagre – £27 a week – and jobs were difficult to get. So we'd sign on but work anyway, that's how people survived. I think a lot of people did that. And then you did all the other stuff you wanted to do, like the tape/slide project and various night classes. I lived on lentils and shopped in charity shops!

WK: I was on the dole, which made life a bit hard, particularly in the winter when I couldn't afford heating at home. During the period I was involved in the newsreel, I began squatting, at first on the Downs Estate and later in Dalston. This made life a little bit more pleasant, as I could live in better places as a squatter than I could afford as a renter. I also did voluntary work for the Advisory Service for Squatters, giving people practical and legal advice about squatting and tenancy.

Neil Martinson (photographer and Centerprise worker): Back in the 1970s. Hackney was very, very run down. I grew up on Clissold Road opposite what is now Stoke Newington School. Where Stoke Newington School is, that whole row was empty houses, all of it – eighty or ninety empty houses, can you imagine? – which was great because we used to go and play in them. Often the people had moved out and left stuff, so we found what we thought was treasure. Actually it was junk.

KB: Oh yeah, at the time [the 1980s] there was a huge amount of empty space. And there wasn't much money, the boom hadn't started.

BB: There were cycles of poverty, people never got out of it, and what was happening with the dismantling of the state was they were never, ever, going to get the chance to get out of it.

EM: Everybody spoke to each other, you know, people got on, you didn't feel that isolated and alone. It was easier to talk to people, to say hello and this and that: 'Where do you live?' 'Ah, over there, OK…' There was a lot of community type of spirit, working man's cafe spirit. A lot of

Below
Pavement car workshop
outside Clarissa House on
the Stonebridge Estate,
Haggerston, which was
demolished in 1985

Left
Clothing factory

Below
Light engineering workshop

*Both from 'One Day
In Hackney' newsreel,
13 December 1983*

people used to go to Centerprise and sit, sometimes for hours, just chatting, nowhere to go. Because when we leave those places, it was back on the street, either Sandringham Road or walking around, you know. There was basically not much to do, and in them times people didn't have tellies. A lot of the younger people were squatting. So it's not like they could go home and watch TV or go home and play music and whatnot.

KB: Diasporas are interesting, because as people move out so other immigrant groups move in, and Hackney's always been that way: as one group moves on, the space becomes open for the next group to move in. I think it makes Hackney a very unusual place.

BB: Well, the representation of Hackney in the mainstream was that you were going to get mugged or stabbed at any point just walking down the street… I think Hackney was represented as if the whole place was one massive sink estate, but actually it wasn't! I felt perfectly safe, nothing ever happened to me anywhere, everybody used to go out late at night.

Guy Farrar (photographer and Centerprise worker): It was fantastically vibrant, active, a lot of social movements, lots of people campaigning for change – pretty white in my experience, but that was changing as well. I know it's a cliché, but it was that melting pot of class, culture, race and ethnicity, and people were trying to find ways to live differently. Post '68, there were people still informed by those revolutionary politics, trying to live some of that out in a much more antagonistic, difficult time.

EM: There was no fairness, a few had a lot and a lot didn't have nothing. Even housing you had to fight. Oh, yeah, because we all was feeling the depression. That's the only word that I can use. We all was going through the same thing. And then we were meeting all the different people, different walks of life, different nationalities, and we were helping each other.

FH: At its best, there was a tangible community spirit that existed in Hackney. It's interesting that Shoreditch always felt like another country, I think it was partly because of the existence of the NF [National Front] down there. But in Hackney Central and Hackney North there was a very strong feeling of community. It was probably the strongest sense of community I've ever had anywhere.

NM: We were out pretty much every weekend on some anti-fascist stuff in Shoreditch, in Brick Lane. There was a kind of ritual every Sunday, getting down to Brick Lane before the fascists did, seeing that you took over the street corners before they did.

DP: I remember Hoxton because we used to go to the market. I remember the NF, they used to have their flags and we were, you know, in shock, and they were outside the Jewish bagel shop, and we were thinking, 'How is that possible?' I do remember Hoxton for that. It never happened at Ridley, but in Hoxton it did.

BS: Nowadays I follow lots of things on Twitter about Hackney, and you look at them and you just think, 'God didn't it look like a dive?' What an awful hole Shoreditch was. You just think… it was awful! You wouldn't

go down Bethnal Green or around there. on certain days. I remember the skinheads every Saturday coming up to Dalston from Bethnal Green. So quite often we'd have all the NF stuff going on and big protests against that...

There was Rock Against Racism and all the anti-racist stuff... that was another thing we took pictures of: we'd all be out there taking pictures, maybe like the clash at the end.

TM: The Tory government was a very disempowering time. I didn't feel like I had access to power, or a voice. And the only way to get back at them and have a voice was to do things ourselves. We did it ourselves with the tools that we had, and there weren't that many tools that we did have! So we'd graffiti, or protest, or organise it ourselves.

Above
Stoking the furnace
at Shoreditch Baths
'One Day In Hackney'
newsreel, 13 December 1983

Left
Works canteen, London
Transport bus garage

Opposite
Public laundry

Beginnings

The Claimants Union and the Unemployed Centre protest against the proposed visit of Specialist Claims Control Unit Members (SCCUM) to Hackney. The picket also called for the Industrial Misconduct Rule to be scrapped and for a guaranteed minimum wage

Both photos from the 'DHSS Arcola Street Picket' newsreel, 22 October 1984

The Industrial Misconduct Rule meant that
if you were sacked your benefit was cut by
forty per cent. SCCUM targeted single mother
claimants: if they could prove a woman was
cohabiting her benefit could be stopped. They
watched to see who visited, they followed
people and made intrusive visits to see if men's
clothes were on the ironing board or hanging
on the washing line. The picket was partially
successful and the SCCUM visit to Hackney
was called off

Funk The Wedding

In Clissold Park, on the day of Prince Charles and Lady Diana's wedding in 1981, members of the Stoke Newington Anti-Nazi League organised Funk the Wedding in support of Rock Against Racism.

NM: You must know that phrase, 'If you can remember it, you weren't really there'? I can't remember it that well, I just remember running around like crazy trying to get it organised, it was an insane thing for just four of us to do, you know, we had no resources, no money, we just chucked stuff in the back of the van get it there, you hope somebody does what they're supposed to do. It was just non-stop craziness, we had no idea if it was going to work at all.

Nobody had done anything like that before in Clissold Park and on the morning we had all the stallholders coming in. I think for some reason we bought a thousand rolls that my mum looked after in her flat. It was just crazy stuff, we were driving around delivering things. And then waited to see if anyone was going to turn up, because if they didn't we were in deep shit, we would have lost a lot of money.

FH: I really don't know where those Funk The Wedding photos came from? I started in 1982!

1983

NEWS

ROUND UP

The Death of Colin Roach

On 12 January 1983, Colin Roach, a 21-year-old black man, was found in the foyer of Stoke Newington police station, dead from a gunshot wound to the mouth. The official explanation was suicide but there were numerous irregularities in the account of what happened. The fight for justice marked the local community's relationship with the police for more than a decade.

Benjamin Zephaniah (poet, musician and activist): I was actually just down the road when it happened and I was amongst the first people to gather outside the police station. In those days we did a lot of demonstrating outside police stations, usually demanding that someone be released…

Just after the death of Colin I wrote 'Who Killed Colin Roach'. It's a rather simple poem but it was written for chanting at demonstrations rather than reading in the comfort of your home, but even when I performed it at readings a large section of the audience would always join in with me.

Who killed Colin Roach? A lot of people
*   want to know*
Who killed Colin Roach? Dem better
*   tell de people now,*
what we seek is the truth, youth must
*   now defend de youth*
Who killed Colin Roach? Tell de people now.
Murder, murder, some a shout
Some of you might have your doubts
But what about our liberty,
*   we want public enquiry…*

Alan Denney (Hackney resident): We were getting ready to go to work and the 8 o'clock news on the radio said that a man had been found shot dead in Stoke Newington police station during the night. Knock at the door, it was a policeman from Stoke Newington police station come to tell us that our stolen car had been found.

'What happened at the station last night, officer?'

'I can't tell you, it's under investigation…' He broke into a laugh: 'But I can tell you the cleaner wasn't very happy.'

Opposite
The Hackney Gazette reports
the death of Colin Roach,
Kingsland High Street,
January 1983

CLR James visits Hackney

In 1983, CLR James, the Trinidadian Marxist revolutionary, pan-Africanist and historian addressed the Hackney Black Alliance at Hackney Town Hall. In 1985, Dalston Library was renamed in his honour, after a campaign to better connect library services with local people.

CLR James: The Caribbean people have shown that over the last thirty or forty years in England is a great gap in the literary field and they have come in. If you are writing the history of English in the last forty years you have to bring in the Caribbean writers...

AD: Somebody, I forget who it was, organised a group of black students from Hackney College to go to local libraries and say 'I need books about where my people come from, from Ghana, Jamaica, Guyana.' And they were told, 'Ah no, we haven't got any actually.' Gradually the library policy changed, to purchase books that reflected the background of the people who lived here, and that was good.

Mackenzie Frank (community librarian):
As a consequence of the dearth of information in society, in institutions, and of course because of institutional racism, black people were being, as it were, kept as second-class citizens in British society. We believed that the only way you are going to destroy racism is by people having clear and honest information about the different cultures, the different races of people that occupied British society, and that was our position. Now, I became aware of the librarian job in an advert in one of the national newspapers, and I was struck by the fact that they were advertising that Hackney was a 'Socialist Borough'... I was wondering if it was a communist republic in east London.

Above
Mackenzie Frank

Opposite
CLR James
Both photos from the 'CLR James at the Black Alliance Town Hall Meeting' newsreel, 29 October 1983

This page and opposite, above
'Stoke Newington Festival 1983' newsreel

Opposite, below
Anti-apartheid badges, ANC and SWAPO flags on Hackney Downs
'Hackney Festival' newsreel, 21 June 1983

The Save Hackney campaign

FH: Hackney felt incredibly under threat. Everything that was going on in government policy seemed to be working against the benefit of Hackney people. The Save Hackney campaign raised the profile of Hackney, and possibly achieved something that was of value to the community One of the people who was coordinating was Heather McAdam, who was seconded from Cultural Partnerships, so she brought a very creative style to it. That long picnic table outside the town hall, you know, all that kind of thing, and it was an artist who designed the logo with the lifebelt. Art serving politics was something I felt very enthusiastic about.

GF: There was a political charge, you know, in the issues around childcare, non-conventional families, non-conventional ways of living – and then there was a conventional council nursery service and the council trying to save money.

What I remember is the taking of the Town Hall chamber by the 'Hackney Under Fives'. It was just very grassroots... I think these nursery workers and parents thought 'We're going to go to lobby our councillors on the town hall steps,' and I don't know how it happened, but they must have thought, 'This isn't good enough, we need to get in there and make some noise!' It was a peaceful ruckus, you know, I remember banners and placards and we were in the council chamber, and I thought, 'What the hell?!'

EM: There was issues around childcare: a lot of black and ethnic minority women wanted to go to work, but they couldn't get their child in a nursery. Lots of nurseries were set up, and playgroups, which enabled a lot of women to either go college or find employment, to improve their skills in one way or the other.

TM: So, you know, the idea of saving Hackney, we were trying to save something that was really run down and destitute, that desperately needed funding and change, and a much less corrupt council. But I suppose in adversity I wanted to defend this place, even though I knew it was riddled with faults and social problems... I had this feral sense of wanting to defend it because I was defending my stories and the place where I grew up, the place where I have memories. But on the other hand, it's easy to romanticise, because Hackney really was not a kind of glorious place, where everything was great and we all loved it. It was shabby, dangerous and genuinely a place of poverty, with multiple occupancy dwellings, and stabbings, not the bijou, bourgeois place it is now.

Opposite, above
Andreas Michaelides, community activist, is interviewed by an RTSNG reporter

Opposite, below
The Hackney Breakfast Show organised by Save Hackney, outside the Town Hall

Both from the 'Save Hackney Campaign – Hackney Breakfast Show' newsreel, 11 December 1983

Hackney Health Emergency

*The German, the Metropolitan, the Mothers'
and St Leonard's Hospitals all closed in
the 1980s. Hackney Health Emergency was
an umbrella organisation for trade unions
and community groups campaigning for
better health services in Hackney.*

TM: Politics was not happening on your
computer screen, via Facebook, in some
distant abstract way. It was happening
right in front of you. The Poll Tax riot, the
boarded up shops and homes, the fierce
cuts to services. Very very poor people
were right in front of our noses when we
queued up to see films at the Rio, slums
just a few streets down.

GF: The Hackney Health campaign was
progressive. It was about preventative
health as well as saving the hospitals.

BB: We went to a lot of demos. There were
demos literally every other day of the week
in those days. There was just so much to
protest about because so much was being
dismantled. The state was effectively
being dismantled, and it was the only
way that anybody could register any
discontent, or that this wasn't right.

**Colin St Leger (teacher, briefly working
with the RTSNG):** The issues and protests
were all merged because of the politics –
the interconnected nature of things was
obvious – so the Inner London Education
Authority [ILEA], the GLC, the miners'
strike, public transport, they weren't
separated from each other.

Above and opposite
*'Hackney Health Emergency
Motorcade' newsreel,
26 September 1983*

Right
A protestor is removed after
occupying St Leonard's A&E
department

M11 Link Road Protest

The RTSNG documented episodes of a decades-long local battle to stop a road-widening plan to link inner London to the new M11 motorway. On this occasion they beat the TV news to the protest, and sold ITV their pictures.

Rebecca Brueton (local seven-year-old, pictured): I remember we went down really early. We waited for the cars to stop and crossed at the front. Someone else started crossing and then we all crossed back again, and back again, and it worked!

BS: Graham Road up to Highbury, up to Holloway, full of juggernauts! Protestors would lie down in the road and stop the traffic. We covered lots of the action with that group.

Well, it quietened the road down! You're free to cycle now. Although people still moan, they don't know what it was like back then when you had to cycle with the juggernauts. God, it was a nightmare.

RB: As a child you're used to there being rules and, you know, when you break the rules, you're in trouble. That taxi driver was definitely breaking the rules, trying to get through us, and in the photos I think I can see the very moment when that happened – there's a picture of the taxi, and there's my little face and this look of shock. I'm looking at him like it was incomprehensible to me that someone could try and push their car through people.

I remember my dad telling me afterwards that we'd been on the radio, and it had said we caused a tailback to Highbury Corner, which seemed like really far away. I was very surprised and proud that we'd done that. I couldn't believe that we had that much effect on the world.

Opposite, above
Seven-year-old Rebecca
Brueton is shocked at a
cabby's driving

Above
Zebra-crossing protests
on Graham Road. MP
Brian Sedgemore and local
councillors Anthony Kendall
and Brynley Heaven are among
the protestors

*All photos from 'M11 Link Road
protest – Graham Road'
newsreel, 1983*

Cultural organisations

The late 1970s and early 1980s saw a flourishing of cultural organisations thanks to funding from the GLC and others. Spending cuts later on made subsidising these groups impossible and most of them disappeared.

EM: I think there was a government incentive to help what they called the disadvantaged boroughs, and Hackney was one of them. They started to plough in a lot of money to help community groups provide services for themselves...

So there was a lot of elderly black luncheon clubs, Turkish, Greek and Indian organisations springing up and, basically, you had to follow the format of the whole society: get a management committee, set up yourself, get your grants filled up. They used some of the money to employ

community workers who then helped black and ethnic minorities to apply for these funds and set up their projects... but then they wanted to tell you how to run your project, what to do. So a lot of people felt it was like a tokenistic gesture and it wasn't their money.

Fern Presant (later RTSNG member):
Adult education was very instrumental in realising that people needed to get out and needed to go to luncheon clubs for their mental health. I remember cycling from place to place to place all through Hackney. There were loads of luncheon clubs in those days doing reminiscence groups. That was always amazing, talking to older people who lived in Hackney all their lives. So many stories. I saw it as an interconnected web.

Adult Education

Aside from the RTSNG, which was directly funded by Hackney Adult Education Institute money earmarked for unemployed people, there were many adult education projects working with older people or minority groups. These were an important community lifeline in the early/mid 1980s, but suffered under Tory cuts. These photos are from a later newsreel, 'Adult Education – too much to lose', dated 1987 or 1998.

Julia Bard in *The Morning Star* on the *Hackney Pensioners Press*:

What they brought was knowledge of how to get things done, courage derived from a lifetime of political struggle, an understanding of how to work collectively, and a burning anger at injustice.

But when they left our untidy office in pre-gentrified Dalston and got on the bus to go home, these marvellous, independent-minded, articulate people were invisible.

Just old ladies with shopping bags. No one suspected that, along with food from the market, those bags contained copy to be edited, proofs to be read, page plans and lists of ideas for forthcoming issues of the paper.

No one imagined that they had just come from a fiery discussion sharing their life experiences as Jews, African Caribbeans, Irish, Indians, English – thrashing out their ideas on pensions, housing, the health service, public transport, international affairs, religion, grandchildren, loneliness, relishing their continuing role in changing the world.

Clovis Julien (mechanic and adult education teacher, pictured overleaf):

I was working for BT Fleet as a motor vehicle mechanic, and running workshops as a supervisor. So during the day I was running workshops for BT Fleet, and as soon as work finished I went straight to the evening classes!

It was something I always wanted to do. Maureen Taylor [of HAEI] asked me to run a women-only class. I knew with the mixed class that some were feeling a little bit uncomfortable, they felt they might be put down by the men – you had the odd one who used to, you know, make funny kinds of remarks. The women's class was very, successful. Some of the classes we had up to twenty women around one car.

When we moved to Kingsland School, the facilities there were excellent. They had scale models! You had various parts of the car, you know, the engine section, the gearbox section, suspension, everything. It made my job easier and it was much more enjoyable for the women. They could actually see it – not just through a crowd around a car – everything was exposed to them.

It gave me a great opportunity to impart my knowledge to others, because I knew what it was like when I was I wanted to get into the motor vehicle trade. Lots of them actually moved on to Hackney College, or various other colleges within the area, to advance themselves. So some may have ended up turning into mechanics. It was a real opportunity to get into a motor vehicle workshop.

Opposite
Hackney Pensioners Press,
Dalston Lane

1983

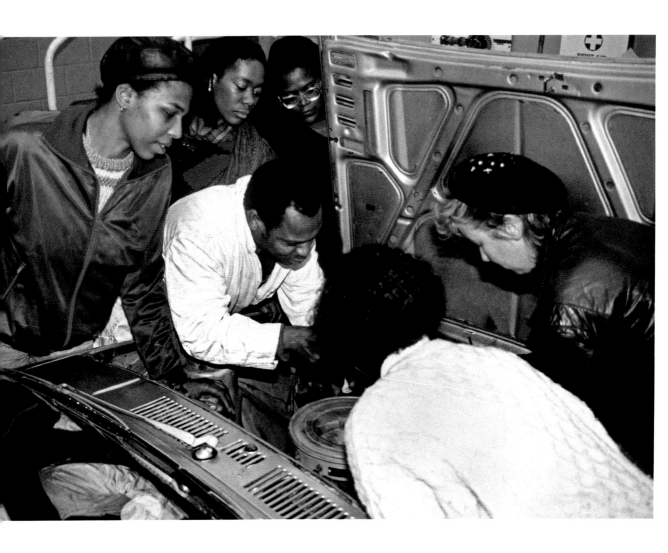

Above
Clovis Julien leading Car
Maintenance for Women
at Kingsland School

Opposite, above
Typing for People with
Disabilities, Alfred Heath
Centre

Opposite, below
Computer class at the
Hackney Information
Technology Centre

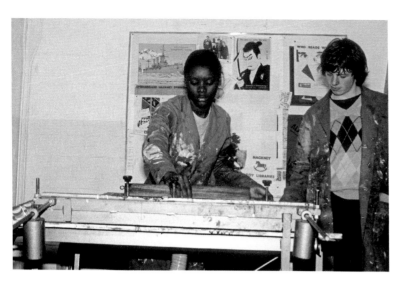

Opposite top
Baluji Shrivastav leads the Indian Classical Music class at Kingsland School

Opposite below
Handicrafts at the Jewish Day Centre, Stamford Hill

Left and below
The Springboard Print Workshop, left, housed at the Lenthall Road Workshop, below, a radical feminist print collective

A festival marked the rehabilitation of shops, workshops and offices to be used by workers' cooperatives on Bradbury Street, Dalston, in 1983. The entertainment included a set by poet John Cooper Clarke

When workers at Queensland
Pleaters, a clothing factory,
asked for better working
conditions they got the sack.
Supported by the National
Union of Tailors and Garment
Workers, they mounted a picket
at the factory gate. Workers
threatened with job losses
in Hackney Council's Direct
Labour Organisation joined
the picket line in solidarity
'Queensland Pleaters' Strike'
newsreel, 23 October 1983

Sandringham Road police incident

28 July 1983: a police stop-and-search with dogs went seriously wrong at the top of Sandringham Road, AKA, the 'Frontline', a meeting place for many in the local black community. The RTSNG captured the escalating situation from the Rio office window. The photos were used by local MP Brian Sedgemore in parliament to argue against the use of dogs in local policing.

FH: The incident at the end of Sandringham Road, yes, I took those photos. The way the police were behaving and were encouraged to behave, it felt like there was a real enemy out there... and everybody, everybody, felt the same. There was stop-and-search... I could spend the rest of the morning listing the things that felt threatening.

EM: There was a bad relationship with the police. Because, as you know, there wasn't many black and ethnic minority police officers, and young black lads were five times more likely to be stopped and searched. There was also a surge of sectioning [under the Mental Health Act section 136] by the police of young black men. They're angry, there's nothing going for them, and when they're stopped and harassed, obviously aggression comes out. And when the police see one young black boy beat up five policemen, they say, 'Oh he must be mad, and instead of taking him to the police station, they take him to the mental hospital. There was a lot of discontentment, a lot of frustration in them times.

TM: It was a very, very heavy time. The stop-and-search and 'sus' laws were unreal. If you saw a group of black guys on the corner you knew that within a couple of minutes they'd be surrounded by shit loads of policemen. It's one of those things it's hard to imagine, but the pressure and the harassment of young black boys, particularly, was very intense and very routine... in our squat we lived next door to a family with older teenage sons, who we were mates with. They would tell me what they went through, and it was off the scale, on a daily basis. The assumption was that any young black man was guilty of something, in the eyes of the police. I'd cycle past the police station on Stoke Newington High Street, knowing that inside police men were beating up black men, and on occasion killing them.

Cat Thomas (Miners' Support Committee member): They were terrifying, the police in Hackney. They used to walk down the High Street with an Alsatian, two of them. They may have been scared, but they were terrifying. It would never have crossed your mind to go to them for help.

Down in the ghetto where the cowboy comes from,
Contentment is something so hard to find,
Every day you wake up and say:
What you gonna do with yourself today,
But deep in your mind you know that you are only wasting your time:
Going down to the same old Frontline,
Down in the ghetto where the cowboy comes from,
A heavy burden always clouds the mind,
Every day you wondering, wondering,
What you gonna do:
Every day you sing the same old song too.
'Down in the Ghetto', Eveline Marius, 1982

On July 28th 1983, an incident took place opposite the Rio, involving the arrest of young black people and the use of Police dogs. The Rio Slide Newsreel caught this incident, and had it up on the screen 24 hours later. Below is a contemporary newspaper account of the event, and the comments of the Chair of Hackney's Police Committee, Brynley Heaven, reproduced from CAMERAWORK.

Hackney

COMMUNITY POLICING STARTS TO BITE

For several weeks Stoke Newington police had been trying out a new tactic, the use of dogs to intimidate the black people they stop and search. Then, on the afternoon of 28 July in Kingsland High Street and Sandringham Road, things came to a head in a way that showed the police using a situation, provoked by themselves, to practice their crowd control techniques.

A young black man had given his savings book to a woman friend. Seeing this, and no doubt 'assuming' it was stolen, two policemen with their dogs stopped and searched her. One of the Alsatians was let free to sit on the corner as shoppers including children walked by. As the police were searching her bag, her friend returned. By this time a police car had arrived and the police tried to put the woman into the back of it, where another unattended Alsatian was sitting. Two police grabbed the man and forced him into a display cabinet!, breaking the glass.

In seconds a crowd gathered and more police and dogs zoomed in until there were three police vans, three police cars and a dog van. Witnesses described a frightening scene of shrieking sirens, and growling dogs. Then the police let the dogs go at the crowd of onlookers. At least three bystanders – all black – were bitten and had to go to hospital. Eugene Knight was walking to his hairdressing shop when he was attacked by one of the dogs, bitten viciously on the thigh, and told to 'piss off' by the handler. Another man was walking home from work:

'...4 or 5 of them had dogs, one which I know by the name of Ginger (G407) who always harasses black people. As I walked to the corner opposite the Rio cinema a police officer approached me and pushed me several times telling me to move. All of a sudden he let his dog go. It jumped towards me at waist height. If I did not jump back it would have been worse because the dog bit me just above the knee.'

Three people were arrested and charged with deception and theft, obstruction and Actual Bodily Harm.

Was it coincidence that the local *Hackney Gazette*, out just that morning, had a picture of the police dog unit under the headline 'Nothing Menacing About these Dogs...Unless, of Course, You Happen To Be A Burglar, Pilferer or Bag Snatcher'. That afternoon showed there is everything menacing about the dogs...especially if you are black.

The Stoke Newington and Hackney Defence Campaign responded by producing a bulletin and distributing it around the area the next day; by arranging a showing of slides taken of the event to those involved and local youth; by taking up the issue at the Saturday street meetings in nearby Ridley Road; and by helping with the legal defence of those arrested. At least two of those bitten are taking legal action against the police.

see photos on page 4

Charles Bolton

Above and opposite
The Rio's annual report in 1983 printed excerpts from the local press and *Camerawork* magazine that used RTSNG photos, to prove the group's impact

COMMUNITY POLICING STARTS TO BITE

Below is a sequence of photographs showing the police with their dogs provoking the people of Stoke Newington: see page 1.

Police with dogs: stop and search...

...the man is grabbed by police

and forced into glass showcase.

A second man is arrested...

dog handlers face down Sandringham Road and set the dogs on the crowd.

BH: The Rio's work is fantastic.   It's centrally loc-
ated for Hackney people, and people who are not directly involved in cultural and political activity can get
to it and see this kind of material [the video, WHO
KILLED COLIN ROACH]: for example, the Rio kept its doors
open all through the uprisings of June and July 1981.
They worked as a refuge, meeting place, first aid and
legal centre.   Their photos taken recently of the use
of dog patrols in Hackney have provided local MP Brian
Sedgemore with valuable ammunition for the campaign to
remove dogs from local policing.   The video combines
with their work: very good and very useful and effect-
ive.

Above
Another stop-and-search with
dogs of a young black man on
Kingsland High Street, 1983

Right and below
The Voice, the only national
black British newspaper, was
set up in Hackney in 1982. In
the run-up to the 1983 election,
it printed a full-page ad for
the Conservative Party, which
featured a photo of a man in a
suit with the caption: 'Labour
says he's black. Tories say he's
British.' Local people were
quick to show their outrage.
*'The Voice Picket, Mare Street'
newsreel, 1983*

Stop the City

On 26 September 1983, the first Stop the City anti-capitalist event brought anarchic mayhem to the City of London and provoked a heavy police response.

WK: The one which really sticks in my mind is Stop the City. Why? I dunno, I guess it was fun, I was an anarchist, and I liked the fact that people were apparently hitting back at a society based on greed and selfishness. Stop the City was effectively a low-key riot in the City of London.

CT: It was terrifying, actually, Stop The City, because of the horses. We thought we were going to get trampled at one point, it was the most frightened I've been at any demonstration. I think we were on the steps of Mansion House or the Bank. Very scary. I don't know if police have got smaller or if I've got bigger, but they seemed so big then, as well as nasty. They all seemed to be guys.

BS: I'd be like, 'I have a right to be here, so get out the way!' Elbow up to the front, take a picture! I didn't care who they were, you know.

It was like that at Stop The City – we'd be up there, taking pictures with the best of them with their big cameras and we'd be with our little Olympuses and Prakticas. There wasn't any fear. We'd go, 'I'm as good as you, move over!'

I remember climbing up statues, climbing up things and taking pictures of the Bank of England and the Stock Exchange.

SH: I think the newsreel group looked a pretty scrappy bunch to be honest. We didn't have bags of cameras or professional-looking equipment. No khaki jackets with masses of pockets and lenses left, right and centre. We were just a motley bunch of mixed-age, mixed-race, mixed-everything really, all sorts. We sometimes travelled in a group but more often than not were just out there and not very noticeable. So we didn't ever get into any grief, that I remember anyway.

Opposite, below
Bank of England officials survey the protestors from the Bank steps

All photos here and overleaf from the 'Stop The City' newsreel, 26 September 1983

One Day in Hackney

FH: I think 'One Day in Hackney' was the start of it. I think I dreamt it up as a community project: coming from a community arts background, I was trying to think of things we could get up on the screen that were community-related alongside the mainstream programme.

The idea was very much, 'Let's show Hackney to Hackney.' I don't remember the moment I thought it up and getting people involved. Well, we advertised it on screen, I imagine. We probably handed out leaflets, we badgered people, we advertised through the community group networks and political networks. I noticed a few Hackney councillors among the names of people who contributed, and it did get a fantastic response. I mean, you've got the credits that show that 'One Day In Hackney' – and even more 'One Day Off In Hackney' – involved forty or fifty people.

We gave a film to everybody involved, they went out, they brought the films back and we put them in a large carrier bag and went to Boots with them. I think we had a little editorial team that put it together.

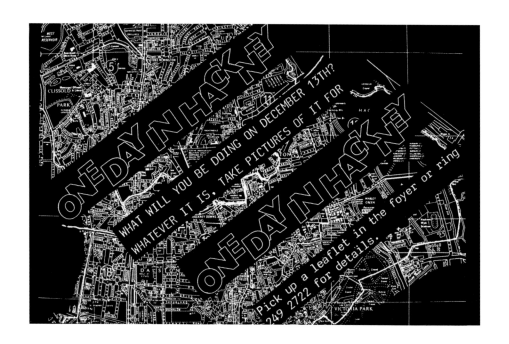

1983

Above
Fishing on the River Lea
at Springfield Park

Opposite
Further south on the river, a
breaker's yard in Hackney Wick

1984

NEWS
ROUND UP

The first anniversary of Colin Roach's death, 12 January 1984

Ngoma Bishop (activist with the Roach Family Support Committee): The family were quite clear what their position was. They wanted to know what happened to their son. They did not say 'This person killed him, that person killed him' – because they couldn't have known that, because they weren't there... Different people had different approaches to it. People were shouting, 'The police killed him, we demand justice!' 'Murderers!' We thought, that may well be what we think personally, but that's not going to help their cause. The family were quite clear: what they wanted was an enquiry into the death of their son.

We formed a committee, organised a campaign and press conference, and we invited, in good faith, all the press. We managed to get people onside like lawyer Tony Gifford, Ken Livingstone and poet Benjamin Zephaniah. And we quickly established links with what was called the Newham Eight, a group of people who had had issues with the police, or the police had had issues with them. We worked with a group called the Southall Sisters and some of the miners from up north, so when we held our press conference, we were well briefed; even though we were inexperienced, we weren't stupid, we knew what we were doing.

Along came the *Daily Mail* the next day, and their reporting bore no relation to anything whatsoever that happened, nothing that we had said. The worst thing about it, we were portrayed as puppets. Because, clearly, as essentially a black campaign, we couldn't have had the wherewithal or intelligence to put together something. So, clearly, we had been manipulated by communists. Well, it almost sounds like Hoover or something, McCarthy. We had to have been manipulated...

With the guidance and involvement of the Roach family, we focused on obtaining an enquiry. We petitioned two subsequent home secretaries, Willie Whitelaw and Leon Brittan, but they gave us no truck. So we said okay, we will establish our own enquiry, and we did it. We commissioned our own enquiry, with help from the GLC, but, like a lot of things, if it's done from the grassroots upwards it kind of goes under the radar.

When you hear about deaths in custody, you very rarely hear Colin Roach's name referenced...

Later, we argued against the police precept: we argued that it was totally irrational that we be paying them – who are not acting in our interests – precepts out of our wages. They are, furthermore oppressing us, killing us, or at the very least ensuring that we didn't find out how he died. I had not long ago joined the Labour Party, so part of my role was to put that argument to the various wards in the borough, mainly Hackney North. So, as black sections and groups within the Labour Party, we came up with this line: 'The council shall have no links with the police unless and until there is an independent public enquiry.' This was after the government had twice turned down our demand for a public enquiry or judicial review. And, surprise – at least to a lot of people – Hackney did adopt it. So for a period of time there was a situation where Hackney Council did not have any links with the police.

One of the protests
demanding justice for Colin
Roach. Initially, many were led
by the Roach Family Support
Committee. Later, the Stoke
Newington and Hackney
Defence Campaign also
campaigned for justice

Hackney Campaign against the Police Bill

The Police Bill proposed extending the police's search powers which, it was widely felt, were used disproportionately against black communities, and in particular young black men, in discriminatory, sometimes violent, ways. On 9 March 1984 a fundraising night for the campaign was held at Chats Palace in Homerton, featuring Benjamin Zephaniah (pictured), Michael Rosen (see Foreword, p 7) and others. On 19 May, Hackney Stop the Police Bill campaigners – and RTSNG reporters – joined a wider demonstration in central London

All photos from 'Hackney Campaign against the Police Bill at Chats Palace' newsreel, 9 March 1984

Anti-apartheid protests

Right
The RTSNG at work at the demonstration on London's South Bank against PW Botha, the South African leader. Margaret Thatcher would receive Botha at Chequers, a major breach of the international isolation of the racist apartheid regime
*'Anti-Botha Demonstration'
newsreel, 8 June 1984*

Opposite
Barclays Bank was a
substantial investor in
apartheid-era South Africa.
Here, protestors call on local
people to boycott the Barclay's
branch at Dalston Junction
*'Anti-Apartheid Demo at
Barclays Bank' newsreel,
9 March 1984*

Above
The week-long picket of the
South African embassy before
Botha's arrival
*'Anti-Apartheid-Anti-Reagan'
newsreel, 15 June 1984*

THE RIO

BRITISH PREMIERE OF JACQELINE AUDRY'S 'OLIVIA' 29 SEPT- 4 OCT

VIDEO PROJECTION SCREENINGS

'WHO KILLED COLIN ROACH'

thurs 15-wed 28   6.30 admission free

BENEFIT FOR

NO INTERVENTION IN CENTRAL AMERICA

films and speakers sept 4 2.30

HACKNEY HEALTH EMERGENCY FILMS 22-26

FILMS ABOUT EAST LONDON 28th

"IT ALWAYS RAINS ON SUNDAY"

"SPARROWS CANT SING"

NEW EXTENDED PROGRAMME

The radical Rio – the people's cinema of Hackney

Andew Woodyatt

'This is the city, in the city there are many stories, and the Rio is one of these.'

Rio Cinema Annual Report, 1982

The Rio in the 1980s was a radical space. It was the UK's first community-run cinema – something unique in a pre-multiplex era, when cinemas were either traditional old-school Odeons and ABCs or arthouse cinemas that were very much the preserve of film buffs and the liberal elite. It was – and still is – run as a non-profit charity.

Its story began in 1977, when a disparate group of punks, hippies, writers, artists, socialists, philanthropists, film buffs and dreamers decided to create Hackney's first arts centre, a utopian creative hub that could be a safe space to champion ideas and causes, as well as a home to diverse community groups and minority voices.

Christine Jackson was a member of the cooperative that founded the Rio. Having worked with Joan Littlewood at the Theatre Royal Stratford, she wanted to apply the same independent spirit in Dalston and build a true community space. 'We want to ensure that at least once a month there will be something in our programme to appeal to everyone,' she wrote, around that time. 'Everyone is working here because they want to. We hope this will create a welcoming atmosphere where people feel they are coming to "their" cinema.'

That this quote comes from an article in the *Observer*, shows the national news-worthiness of a new cinema opening, at a time when most were closing and replacing films with bingo.

The only other cinemas in London to offer something different were the Electric Film Club in Portobello Road and the Scala in King's Cross. They screened cult films, midnight movies and eclectic all-nighters

Opposite
Rio programme poster, September 1983. Isaac Julien's film *Who Killed Colin Roach?* was commissioned by the Roach Family Support Committee

that appealed to the nocturnal counterculture – a crowd of anarchists, freaks, hedonists, students and hardcore film buffs. While the Rio shared some elements of this in its programming, it was also so much more: its political values and its equality manifesto meant it would be a unique social experiment that was way ahead of its time.

The current vogue for neighbourhood indie cinemas with diverse, inclusive aims? The Rio has been doing that for over forty years.

The Rio before the Rio

To set all this in context, in Hackney in the 1970s, times were very, very tough. Unemployment was high (though not as high as it would be in the 1980s), and sections of the population were drifting out of the borough. Entire streets were derelict, even the railway stations had closed. In its heyday, Hackney had been home to fifty-two cinemas – with sixteen of them in Dalston and Stoke Newington alone. But one by one, these were shutting up shop.

The early 1970s was a low point for British cinema. As attendances sank, revenue for films also dropped, and for every Hollywood or British blockbuster there were a hundred dreadful low-budget films which did nothing to halt the decline. This was the era of the *Carry On...* films and big-screen adaptations of TV hits, like the *On The Buses* movies. Many London cinemas diversified to focus on Kung Fu, Bollywood and Blaxploitation titles.

However, the Rio (or the Classic as it was then called) went in a different direction.

In 1970, a relaxation in the censorship laws allowed cinema clubs to show uncensored adult entertainment – porn, in other words. The Classic cinema chain had operated on Kingsland High Street since 1937 and was looking for ways to adapt to, or to create new audiences. The building had already housed a news theatre, a cartoon palace and a continental arthouse cinema... it was time for the Classic to go grindhouse.

So, with a name change to the Tatler Cinema Club, it threw open its doors to customers its advertising referred to as 'Sophisticated, un-shockable, with-it cinemagoers.' Showing sexploitational, hardcore double-bills of films like *Truck Stop Women*, *Sisters in Leather* and the charmingly titled *Use the Back Door*, the Dalston Tatler proved to be one of the most successful porn cinemas on the circuit. Its Vegas-style live striptease and burlesque starred professional performers with names like Desiree, Voluptua and Velvet, who also danced at notorious Soho clubs like The Windmill. As shown in the film *Gypsy* (1962, starring Natalie Wood and Rosalind Russell), all strippers had a gimmick; one such gimmick at the Tatler was a twelve-foot python, which kept warm in a basket on top of the projector in between shows.

Outside its doors, meanwhile, Hackney was downtrodden – divided less into 'haves' and 'have nots' than into 'have nots' and 'have nothings' – but the resilient and resourceful East End community didn't allow this to grind them down. It was a melting pot of left-wing politics, solidarity and experimentation, a haven for those who rejected the traditional values of the West End theatre or bourgeois film, music, art and writing. Many in the staunchly working-class communities worked together to make their lives better.

One of these community hubs was the Centerprise bookshop. This was a grassroots workers' collective and a hotbed of resistance, home to a uniquely diverse selection of books, a café and small meeting rooms, where many classes took place and where underground groups met.

With so many local residents wanting to hold meetings and classes, space was always an issue... which brings us back to the Rio.

By 1975, things were looking terminal for the now-renamed Classic (which was just over the road from Centerprise), and the management announced they were thinking of closing. This created a buzz among locals, who saw the cinema as a potential community arts space.

In April 1976 a local businessman, Paul Theodorou, took over the lease and renamed the cinema. It needed to distance itself from its seedy reputation; 'Rio' was a fairly common cinema name and, more importantly, being only three letters long it cut the costs of replacing the signage.

The Rio opened with a line-up of Kung Fu, Bollywood, Turkish films, and sexploitation and Blaxploitation movies, as well as lots of Elvis musicals. For the first time in ages it was regularly packed, but years of neglect to the fabric of the building demanded expensive repairs:

a leaking roof, knackered projectors, worn-out heating, broken seats and the tatty screen and basic mono sound all urgently needed attention. In 1977, a working group of locals was formed. They were part of the thriving community arts scene in the area, and saw in the Rio a place where Hackney's literacy, education and campaigning groups could use both the cinema and the huge basement spaces.

The working group fought long and hard to raise the funding and in April 1979, thanks to a large grant from the GLC, the Rio officially opened its doors.

But just a month after opening Hackney's arch nemesis, Margaret Hilda Thatcher, swept to power in the 1979 General Election.

Hackney strikes back

The rise of a new kind of populist Conservatism in the UK was mirrored in the US by the election of Ronald Reagan in 1980, a landslide Republican win that marked the beginning of a moral crusade of Christian family values, which would by the end of the 1980s permeate every area of mainstream life.

What sprang up was a culture of opposition: it was an incredibly dynamic moment in the arts, music, fashion and film, as well as a time of protest, of getting educated, of fighting back and challenging authority. And since you weren't going to get anything from the government, it was a time of DIY art: you borrowed, you stole, you photocopied. Low budget often meant no budget, which made artists and film-makers very creative.

In these cooperatives, indie start-ups and grassroots organisations, the legacy of free-loving 1960s hippies meshed with the punk attitude of disenfranchised 1970s youth. Life was exciting on the margins, there was a sense that things could happen, that the old values were being thrown off.

British cinema was having a renaissance too. For the first time since the gritty social realism of the 1970s, a fresh wave of British film-makers were exploring class, gender, race, politics and sexuality. One driver of this was Channel 4, which first broadcast in November 1982 and represented a bold new voice. Less constrained than the BBC, it wasn't afraid to shock – in fact, that was pretty much its main remit in those early years – and it made films for cinema as much as for TV. As early as December 1979, the Rio hosted fundraisers for the fledgling Channel 4 group, which in turn started to commission work by local film-makers, many of whom were Rio regulars.

It was a busy time for the Rio. As well as screening one of the most progressive film programmes of any cinema in London, reflecting the make-up of the local community and celebrating black cinema, queer cinema, feminist cinema and world cinema, it also hosted gigs and

The Tape/Slide group shoots
Trafalgar Square
*'CND Anti-Reagan
Demonstration' newsreel,
9 June 1984*

concerts. It featured many women-only nights, was one of the early
Rock Against Racism venues and staged early Rough Trade gigs by
bands like Stiff Little Fingers, Spizz Energy and Bad Manners – which
may have inspired their song 'Night bus to Dalston'.

The Rio's Kung Fu late-show double bills every Friday quickly
became legendary. The film prints, which travelled around many UK
cinemas, were often badly scratched and in poor condition, but that
didn't matter: the packed crowd at the Rio were mostly too stoned to
notice through the weed haze, which so strongly impregnated the seats
and carpet it would often require the liberal use of air freshener before
the Saturday Kids Club the following morning.

The Rio was a true community cinema, and not only for its films.
Very early on, Thatcher's government made 'Law and Order' a priority, to
keep Middle England Tories happy, but tensions simmered in the inner
cities: poverty, spending cuts, unemployment and police harassment
were the sparks that in the summer of 1981 set off rioting across the
UK – in Toxteth, Handsworth, Moss Side, Brixton and of course Hackney
and Dalston. On the front line in the most deprived borough in London,

the Rio became a community drop-in centre and a refuge and safe house for those caught up in the police violence, as well as a first aid point and a legal advice centre.

Throughout the 1980s, the Rio would play host to fundraisers and benefits for causes including CND, the miners' strike, the ANC Women's Section, Guatemala, the Hasbudak Family Campaign, Nicaragua Solidarity, the Gay Switchboard and Lesbian Line, and the campaign to free Baader-Meinhof member Astrid Proll. The Rio team took an active role in campaigning on women's issues, as well as for lesbian and gay rights – reclaiming the term 'queer' and broadening the umbrella of London's LGBTQ+ community. In the early 1980s, the AIDS crisis began to create an atmosphere of fear and uncertainty. Governments on both sides of the Atlantic were slow to act; reliable information was limited and the tabloids had a field day whipping up homophobic hysteria. One of the Rio's big successes was a fact-based, no-nonsense short film about AIDS, produced by the RTSNG in association with the Terrence Higgins Trust. As well as being shown on the big screen before the main features, this was transferred to VHS and was widely used by community groups and health organisations across the UK.

All these stories shaping life in Hackney were reflected in the films shown at the Rio – as well as the work of the RTSNG. They produced timely reports broadcasting an alternative viewpoint on the miners' strike, CND and the Greenham Common Women's Peace Camp, anti-capitalist demos, deportations, apartheid, racism and police brutality.

From the mid 1980s on, all this activity was overseen by the Rio's most famous staff member, Hackney's most out-there cat, Queenie. In 1984, Hackney was down to its last two cinemas – the Rio and the nearby Ace, When the Ace played the new Clint Eastwood film, *Sudden Impact*, and hardly anyone came to see it, Ray, the manager, wandered over to the pub across the road to drown his sorrows. When he asked the bar staff why no one was coming to see the week's big release, they laughed and pulled a pirated VHS copy from under the bar. Two weeks later, the Ace closed for good and its in-house mouser, Queenie, a sassy cat-about-town, got a promotion to the Rio. Queenie's arrival made the front page of the *Hackney Gazette* and she quickly became an essential member of the team. Legend has it that due to unreliable heating at the time, regular Rio customers brought cat treats to lure Queenie to come and sit in their laps and keep them warm during screenings.

Queenie definitely provided some light relief for everyone at the cinema during this challenging period; the mid 1980s was an inspirational time for British cinema, with pioneering independent directors pushing the boundaries of sex, gender and politics. However, this outraged the tabloid press and the Church, and provided fuel for the Conservatives' moral fire. After Thatcher was re-elected for the second time in 1987, the

Ray Ellis, manager of the Ace Cinema, hands over Queenie the cinema cat to Ruby Collinson, house manager of the Rio in February 1984. This made the front page of the *Hackney Gazette*

Conservatives hardened their campaigns against the Left, the unions and minorities, including the LGBTQ+ community.

Section 28, which was enacted in 1988, banned the promotion of homosexuality in schools and was a particularly nasty piece of legislation. The act was written in a deliberately vague manner, so that any organisation funded by local councils could in effect be prosecuted, and that included spaces like the Rio. The unfortunate truth is that it forced many groups and organisations to self-censor and limit their work. This, combined with the abolition of the GLC, cuts to council and arts spending, the effects of rate-capping, and many other difficulties meant that by the late 1980s many of the activists and protest groups were burning out.

Around 1988, this combination of factors brought an end to the RTSNG, and, as indie film production moved more towards the centre ground, a slightly more mainstream programme of films and events emerged at the Rio.

The early 1990s saw changes in music and fashion. Drug culture took over clubbing, and acid house and rave became the new focus of the counterculture, while the film community suffered the loss of many

GERMANY IN AUTUMN
FREEDOM FOR ASTRID PROLL

Astrid Proll released on bail at the start of her trial in West Germany on Sept 20th.

A CONTROL UNIT developed through U.S. military research has now being used as part of the security apparatus of most "Western Democracies"

Stammheim Top Security Prison where Andreas Baader, Gudrun Ensslin & Jan Carl Raspe were killed Oct 1977.

DALSTON RIO SUNDAY 7TH OCT 3P.M.

iconic creative voices, silenced by AIDS. It also saw a massive expansion of multiplex cinemas across the UK, spelling the end for many of the UK's traditional high-street independents. A few, however, fought back, to become the indies, locals and boutique chains we know today.

Somewhere in the middle of all this, the Rio not only survived, but, barring the odd hiccup, thrived. In 2017, it raised the funds to turn an idea that had first been dreamed up over thirty years ago – the creation of a second screen in the basement – into reality. As work began to clear the space of accumulated junk – old posters, endless boxes of paperwork, old popcorn machines – a battered filing cabinet was unearthed. It contained thousands of slides of Hackney, just as they had been left by the RTSNG in the 1980s, a time capsule with a potent message from the radical past.

With this book, we're proud to recognise this incredible legacy and carry it with us into the future. In 2019, the Rio was voted 'Independent Cinema of the Year', and we are continuing to look for new ways of being the pioneering community resource we've always been.

**Andrew Woodyatt, artist, writer, film-maker and cinema historian
Summer 2020**

The radical Rio

The Tape/Slide Newsreel Group photos in context

Alan Denney

'I'm arguing for an art that documents monopoly capitalism's inability to deliver the conditions for a fully human life.'
Allan Sekula, *Photography Politics: One*, 1979

The archive's rediscovery

The Rio Tape/Slide Newsreel Group's photos are a priceless time capsule of Hackney during the Thatcher years: 10,000 glass-mounted slides and 2,000 frames on film strips, all taken with SLR cameras on 35mm colour slide film between 1981 and 1988.

For thirty years the photos lay forgotten in a grey filing cabinet deep in the bowels of the Rio, until renovation work to create a second screen began in 2016. Without an analogue projector to view the slides it was hard to know what they had found, but one of the Rio's staff, Andrew Woodyatt, realised it was a treasure trove. While Andrew was busy resisting a shameful suggestion from the cinema's board to sell off the filing cabinet and its contents, chance intervened: Tamara Stoll, a local artist and community activist, heard about the archive while she was researching a book on Ridley Road Market, and told me about it.

Over the next two years I digitised the slides and relived my thirties. Every now and again, the scanner would crank out images of Jenny (my wife), friends, colleagues, our juggling neighbours Sue and Eric, familiar events and crowds of half-forgotten faces. When the nostalgia wore off, it was clear that the archive was a unique photographic survey of life in Hackney, a social history of the turbulent 1980s. What makes the archive even more unusual is that the photos weren't taken by white, male, middle-class professional photographers, but by a mixed group of young, unemployed locals who belonged to a community photography project based in the dingy, unheated cellar of the local cinema.

Community activism and education in Hackney

The RTSNG emerged from the radical counterculture that had taken root in Hackney in the late 1960s. Politicised by events in Vietnam and Northern Ireland, and by the poverty, unemployment, racism and sexism at home, many young people in Hackney tuned into the zeitgeist and began imagining a world without capitalism. Some, like the Angry Brigade, were in too much of a hurry, and their bullets and bombs only got them long prison sentences. Others thought you could change society from below: if people organised themselves locally to pursue common interests, they could improve life for themselves – and, even if they didn't achieve their immediate goals, the experience of working together, demanding together, would empower them to keep going back to ask for more. With small grants for community development easily obtainable from the council, the GLC, the GLAA (Greater London Arts Association) and some charities, dozens of community projects and self-help groups sprang up all over Hackney in the 1970s and 80s.

The hub for many of these activities was Centerprise. The community bookshop on Kingsland High Street, opposite the Rio Cinema had books, pamphlets, noticeboards, meeting rooms, legal advice sessions, classes and much more. Hackney Flashers, the Young Photographers Group and the Hackney Unemployed Media Scheme were all based at Centerprise, all taking photographs for posters, postcards, leaflets, the alternative press and travelling exhibitions.

The RTSNG was just one of the offshoots that emerged from the buzz emanating from the lime-green bookshop on Kingsland High Street, but it wouldn't have happened without the Hackney Adult Education Institute (HAEI).

HAEI was absorbing some of the revolutionary ideas about the role of education that were being generated by radical educationalists such as Paolo Freire, Ivan Illich, Richard Hoggart and Chris Searle, writers whose books always sold well at Centerprise. Education wasn't just about exams or making yourself attractive to employers: it could be a liberating force for social change. So HAEI began a move away from traditional evening classes – Pitman shorthand, flower arranging etc – and developed a wide range of classes in partnership with local community groups. In 1982 Maureen Taylor and her (mostly female) colleagues at HAEI provided funding for tutors for twenty-five classes specifically for the unemployed, including: Afro-Brazilian Music, Black Studies, Technical Stage Craft, Mobile Play Construction, Graphics, Working with Children, Women's Self Defence... and the RTSNG.

Ideas in photographic practice

New photographic ideas and practice that were being developed locally provided another underpinning for the RTSNG: the Half Moon Photography Workshop in Bethnal Green, its influential *Camerawork* magazine and books by Jo Spence and Terry Dennett were publicising the methods and theorising the practice of radical photography between 1976 and 1985. *Camerawork* carried articles about community groups using photography in various campaigns to promote social change. It described tape/slide projects in Manchester, Paddington and Blackfriars, and *Camerawork* issue 13 (1979) gave step-by-step instructions for making a DIY tape/slide presentation. In 'The Blackfriars Settlement', an article in that issue, Caro Webb wrote:

> In a society dominated by centralised mass media, tape/slide is an alternative. It can be used to apply political pressure, articulate needs and opinions, and to convey information. Issues and problems in a community can be voiced strongly and coherently by the people directly concerned, which sets tape/slide radically apart from the mass media. Tape/slide makes an important contribution in the struggle of the working class for greater control over their own lives.

Terry Dennett also linked contemporary community photography to earlier examples of agitprop. His research into the Comintern-sponsored Workers' Photography Movement in Britain in the interwar years found a network of Workers' Film and Photo League groups in East London, including one in Dalston that produced images for left-wing newspapers, displays and campaign leaflets.

So, really, the lineage can be traced back at least to the 1930s – and to Germany. In Germany, left-wing dailies and magazines had achieved mass circulation in the years leading up to 1933 in a way they had not in Britain. The demand from these publications for photographs created a new type of photographer: the photo-reporter. When the Nazis took power, some of these photographer-journalists came to London and became the nucleus of a new weekly magazine, *Picture Post*.

From the late 1930s to the early 1950s *Picture Post* would sell up to two million copies a week. It was anti-fascist and pro-welfare state and it introduced Britain to a new format: the campaigning photo-report – a series of photographs together with captions and text arguing the case for free medical care, full employment, slum clearance etc. *Picture Post* held up a mirror so that ordinary people could see themselves at work, rest and play, looking respectable, competent and self assured. Once the welfare state had been created and the Cold War set in, so-called 'Reds' and communist sympathisers in the mainstream media were seen as a liability. *Picture Post* folded and socially engaged photography disappeared forever from Fleet Street.

Thirty years later, it resurfaced on Kingsland High Street in Dalston.

Tape/slides and the birth of the Group

The tape/slide format the RTSNG used was like an analogue version of today's PowerPoint presentations, and was originally developed by the advertising industry in the 1970s. Banks of slide projectors were programmed to display sequences of still images that had been synchronised to a soundtrack. Another important antecedent, the newsreel, had long been part of the programme at most British cinemas. Made, most famously, by Pathé, these were commercially produced short documentary films about topical events that embodied the same colonialist values and patronising tone as the mainstream media. Amazingly, they survived until the 1970s, when TV finally killed them off.

The Rio Tape/Slide Newsreel Group took the advertising-born synchronised projector and the commercial newsreel as templates and subverted them. Using their own voices members put out their own stories, producing previously unseen scenarios of working-class life.

The idea for a tape/slide group in Dalston came from Annette Giles at the HAEI. She approached Sandra Hooper, who was working at

Camerawork magazine, issue 13 (1979), published a description of tape/slide, examples of its use by campaigning groups and a step-by-step guide showing how to make a tape/slide

Margaret Thatcher and
Norman Tebbitt: a slide with
a blunt editorial comment,
made for one of the Save
Hackney newsreels

Centerprise, sometime in the early 1980s: together, they decided that
producing a newsreel would be a good focus for an adult education
group; Felicity Harvest, a coordinator at the Rio, was involved from the
start, and the cinema was happy to provide access to its screen, as
well as a basement meeting space. HAEI employed Sandra Hooper as
a tutor and she became the group's coordinator and facilitator. Good-
quality camera equipment and portable sound-recorders were bought
with grants from various public funds. Unemployed young people were
recruited and the group started meeting once a week, for a couple of
hours on Thursday afternoons. Some forty or so people passed through
the group over its lifespan; some were committed regulars, others came
and went. They were shown how to use the 35mm cameras and tape
recorders, and encouraged to develop their own storylines. Decisions
about which subjects to follow up were taken in group meetings, then
storyboards were drawn up, scripts for the newsreel commentary
were written, tasks were allocated, interviews and shoots were set
up. The resulting images and sound recordings were then edited and
synchronised ready for screening. The finished newsreels were shown
on the Rio's big screen, after the commercial ads and before the main
film, as a regular part of the weekly programme. The group had just one
projector, a Kodak Carousel, to screen their newsreels.

    Over the six years of its existence, the group made at least sixty
newsreels; the average audience at the Rio during that time was around
a thousand people a week. By this reckoning, the group did what it had
set out to do.

The photographs

All the photos were taken with slide film. It's a contrast-y recording medium and it produces richly saturated colours, making images ideal for projection. Considering the basic SLR cameras and the complexity of analogue photography – and developing at least some of the films themselves, in rigged-up darkrooms – the vast majority of the photos are well taken, nicely composed and decently processed. A few of the photos are visually striking, but they weren't trying to make standalone works of art: newsreel photos had to contribute to the narrative. There are very few portraits of individuals: the photographers mainly took groups of people doing things together; most of them are facing the camera. The people photographed look comfortable with the camera pointing at them; very few play up to it. The photos cover a wide range of events and activities: demonstrations and protests, street life, community groups, festivals, urban decay, racism, housing, unemployment, deindustrialisation, recreation, health, education and more.

Since the photos were taken with the intention of telling a story in tandem with an audio commentary, when we look at them now they are not in their original context. Sadly the audiotapes with the commentary, or interviews that the group made, have not been found, so we do not have the full story. Some of the meaning has been lost. Even so, each image is packed with information about Hackney in the 1980s and, with the help of descriptive captions and text, viewers can see the fine detail of Hackney's social fabric – information that isn't recorded anywhere else.

Once the photographs have been catalogued and the collection made searchable, they will be lodged at Hackney Archives where they will be freely accessible to the public.

The end

What's so special about the group's photos? After all, if you Google 'Hackney images' you can find hundreds, thousands, of the same sort of documentary-type photos as the group took: street life, people at work, protests, festivals etc. However, before digital technology and the internet democratised making and distributing images, documentary photography was different. It was – at best – reformist, but mostly it was just illustrating the Establishment imaginary. Photographers were respectable professionals: why would they want to go slumming and, anyway, who would want to look at, let alone pay for, photos of the unwashed poor? The lives of working people just weren't worth recording. From the 1950s until the 1980s it was difficult to find sympathetic representations of working-class Londoners in any medium. There were plenty of reassuring stereotypes – the cheerful-but-stupid Cockney, or the exuberant Carnival-goers dancing with policemen busy pretending they aren't racists – but mostly it was

6.

The Rio Slide/Tape Newsreel Project - The Rio Cinema, London E 8

This project was set up five years ago with the Rio Community
Cinema, a local independent cinema with a management committee
of local people elected each year. The same tutor has worked
on it since its inception and its success is largely due to
her skills and enthusiasm. The centre is also easily accessible
on a busy main shopping street with good bus services.

The cinema already had a slide advertising service for local
groups and cinema staff approached the AEI with the idea of a
project aimed at producing a regular slide/tape local 'newsreel'
which would be projected as a feature along with the main film.
The AEI agreed to fund 3 x 2 hour sessions for a qualified
photography tutor to work with unemployed young people on this
project; a student placement at the Rio concentrated on publi-
city and communications; the cinema provided all the equipment.

As well as introducing young people to the technical skills
involved in using a camera, making recordings, and finally com-
bining these skills in presenting short audio-visual features,
the aim is also to encourage each student to work through a
whole process from decision-making over choice of subject (in
consultation with the group and Rio staff), research into the
subject, script-planning and writing, and actual production.
This has been achieved with a considerable degree of success
and some completed features have appeared on the screen (eg
issues such as Health, AIDS, housing, and currently one on the
proposed abolition of ILEA).

Students are recruited through the prospectus, leafleting, and
contact with other organisations. The numbers involved have been
good, around 15 on the register and an average attendance of
10/11, but recruitment has needed to go on all the time as some
of the earlier students moved on to jobs or training courses.
This turn-over means that new students come in who need to
start at the beginning, and the actual process of putting
together a programme is slower than anticipated. However, as
the main aim is for young people to acquire skills and self-
confidence rather than to create a 'professional' newsreel
unit, this does not matter, so long as the individuals involved
feel they are progressing. The fact that the group works towards
a clearly defined end product that the young people involved
can actually see playing a part in the life of the local community has probably been a factor in the project's success.

P. Maureen Taylor 1988

An internal report by HAEI
manager Maureen Taylor
summarising the project and
supporting an extra year's
funding in 1988
*From Maureen Taylor's
personal archive*

a dreary parade of strikers, football hooligans, drunks, rioters and other criminals. In the Tory media, Hackney was a poverty-ridden slum full of dangerous street people, anarchist squatters, sex/drug fiends and, scariest of all, Black Muggers – all of whom were being encouraged by the borough's 'Loony Left' council. The RTSNG photographers rejected these nasty stereotypes and produced a comprehensive and assertive affirmation of Hackney's working-class identity. When they took photographs of their neighbours in a respectful and empathetic way they were sticking two fingers up at the Establishment and the lies told by its media stooges. The RTSNG, together with their colleagues in other community photography projects, were democratising photography.

While the group was making its newsreels, mainstream documentary photography was changing direction. The humanistic naturalism of *Picture Post* was old hat and street photography, hot from the USA, was becoming the new thing: the heroic lone photographer, risking himself in the urban jungle, using his camera to document all the weirdness of the human zoo for our vicarious entertainment. The language of photography began to change too: these guys no longer took pictures, they went out and captured them. In 1986, while the group was taking photos of Travellers, Pensioners' Health Day and squatters, Martin Parr's book *The Last Resort* became the photographic sensation of the year. Parr, a middle-class man from the Home Counties, photographed overweight, working-class Northerners on holiday in New Brighton, stuffing their faces, surrounded by rubbish and generally not looking good. Parr definitely wasn't following the old-fashioned photograph-as-you-would-be-photographed motto of the RTSNG. Instead, he invited us to share his incomprehension of these awful people. The book made Parr famous (he was said to be Thatcher's favourite photographer) and it helped to popularise street photography in Britain just at the same time as politically engaged community photography was being killed off by Tory cuts.

The last newsreel was made in 1988. Rate-capping had slashed the money available for community projects, the GLC and ILEA no longer existed, and the Left was in retreat. At some point that year Sandra Hooper left for Australia, and she wasn't replaced as coordinator. The Tape/Slide Newsreel Group just petered out.

The group's newsreels didn't spark a proletarian revolution but they did leave us an intimate, encyclopaedic visual survey that explains why and how Hackney stood up to Thatcherism. The group's message to us is that, whatever the circumstances, resistance is never futile.

Alan Denney, Hackney resident
Summer 2020

Opposite
The cover of *Camerawork* magazine, issue 13 (1979)

CAMERAWORK

An accidental double exposure at a photo-kit session at Ranwell Club Playscheme, Bow. Summer 1978.

Photography in the Community

No 13   Half Moon Photography Workshop   50p/$1.50

On the corner of Northwold
and Fountayne Roads

Playing out on Princess
May Road

George Moseley on his stall on
Bradbury Street, just outside
the Kingfisher Cafe, 1984

1984

Friends, Kingsland High Street

The Hasbudak deportation

The Home Office refused to drop its hostility to the Hasbudak family and Mr Hasbudak was deported to Turkey on 12 March 1984. Mrs Hasbudak and the two children then followed on 4 April. Supporters of the family accompanied them to the airport, including Sandra Smidt, head teacher at William Patten School, pictured below with her arm around Fatih Hasbudak

All photos from the 'Hasbudak Deportation' newsreel, April 1984

The annual Hackney Show
on Hackney Downs
Various years/newsreels

Hackney Womyn's Peace Camp

After 30,000 women joined
hands around RAF Greenham
Common at the Embrace The
Base protest in December 1982,
women's peace camps sprang
up in cities across the world.
The Hackney camp in front of
the Town Hall coincided with the
Council's Peace Week in 1983

*'Hackney Womyn's Peace
Camp – Greenham Womyn are
everywhere' newsreel, 1984*

Greenham Common

The RTSNG made multiple trips to cover the Greenham Common Women's Peace Camp protesting about US nuclear cruise missiles at RAF Greenham Common. At the camp were a large contingent of Hackney women. They also covered the Womyn's Peace Camp at Hackney Town Hall and demonstrations at the Houses of Parliament and the US Marines Barracks inl London, producing at least four newsreels.

BS: I went to Greenham Common quite a bit. I hated it, actually – well, I didn't like camping! I was really young and went down with all these women, really ill prepared. I just jumped in the van and said 'I'm coming down to take some pictures and record it.' And it was freezing! I didn't realise you had to dress for the cold, I didn't have the correct clothes or the bedding. So I'd be there drinking black coffee to keep warm, all night, freezing!

DP: I think we talked to some soldiers, in fact, through the fence, and then we were really just there, just taking pictures, it was a nice, supportive, female kind of place, you know what I mean. People were so concerned about the missiles.

BB: The first time I went there was with the newsreel group and I was actually quite embarrassed I'd never been there before. I couldn't believe it when I got there. I couldn't believe that all these women had been living there, I think it was towards the tail end of it when they'd been living there for about two years. I was stunned that they'd sacrificed so much to make the point. And they were utterly dedicated to it.

Both photos from 'Greenham Common 10 Million' newsreel, 5 October 1984

Centerprise reopens

In 1984, Centerprise bookshop reopened after refurbishment.

BS: Centerprise was unique, you don't get that sort of community-based project any more. It was a great place for all – mentally ill people, homeless people, young people such as ourselves – who would have had nowhere to go otherwise. It had many resources: advice, young people's projects, girls' projects, unemployment projects, a bookshop.

You could sit there all day with a cup of tea that cost, what, 10p, nobody threw you out. The older guys had a game of chess, they could sit and play, you could read the daily papers, you could see artists work exhibited on the café walls.

EM: Centerprise was something I never knew before, with a lot of white, middle-class people in there. Well, I'd call them that because they'd just come out of university, working with the underprivileged groups. There was loads of different projects going on in there. So I joined the writing project.

They had a literacy project for people whose reading and writing wasn't that good. People always had this thing about filling in forms, had problems with application forms for housing, application form for doctor, application form for this, that. They had an advice centre that used to help people with immigration matters. A lot of people had immigration problems.

TM: Centerprise was a genuine community hub: there were posters and art works and information about stuff that was going on. It also had a black history section, a black book section.

I think they ran black education Saturday schools, which were common at the time, to supplement the extraordinarily poor white curriculum we still have!

There were a lot of local pamphlets fluttering around. It was all very handmade, you know, you could see the staples. It was fine, someone's mate would draw something and then it would be photocopied or Gestetnered, and there was the pamphlet. Generally, in public spaces, on pub walls, in the high street, there were posters everywhere – about gigs, events, raves, sound systems, black churches, political slogans. This was the era of fly posters and Gestetner and zines.

SH: It was trying to do things differently. It was a group of people all with common aims. Everyone took part in all aspects. Lots of jokes about collective working meaning that everyone had to clean the toilets.

BS: Centerprise sort of gave me a sense of community, of family because I left home really early. I could have been at a loose end. I could have gone anywhere and done anything, but Centerprise and the Rio kept me grounded. It was my triangle: Centerprise, the Rio and the pub.

Opposite, above
Schoolchildren visit Centerprise

Opposite, below
The Trinidad-born American writer Rosa Guy reopens Centerprise bookshop after a refurbishment, June 1984

One Day Off in Hackney

'One Day Off in Hackney' was a follow-up newsreel to the popular 'One Day in Hackney', again featuring multiple contributors, and this time accompanied by a soundtrack featuring poetry by Gail Baker and Eveline Marius. It was produced in August 1984.

When politicians speak of Hackney,
The picture is sad and gloomy
Looking through broken glass down
*   into the city.*
They just give us images of dereliction
*   and pity.*
It's true. The buildings need repair
And Hackney can seem empty and bare.
We wait for them to show they care
But come on down and see the other
*   side of town...*

St Leonard's Hospital closure

Motorcades, demonstrations and the occupation of St Leonard's were all part of the Hackney Health Emergency campaign to protect local health services

All photos from 'St Leonard's Hospital Closure Protest and Occupation' newsreel, 6 July 1984

Kingsland High Street

FH: Most of the shops were occupied as I remember, but they always gave the impression of hanging on by a thread, you know. There were exceptions – the pie-and-eel shop, of course was well known, and a place of pilgrimage for some – and Ridley Road was lively enough, but it never seemed to spill out into the High Street.

TM: I remember it being grim! It was grotty. It was dirty, graffitied, a lot of boarded-up shops… Also that whole thing when shops say they've got, like, flood stock for three weeks only and then they're gone, or where they sell weird suits, or whatever. Am I misremembering this? …

What I can remember is that finding something to eat in the evenings was hard – I cycled everywhere, I was always hungry. There was McDonald's, there were quite a lot of Turkish shops, there were West Indian shops – I used to drink cans of Dunn's River condensed milk, because if you're cycling you need energy quickly – but there weren't these bijou eateries, or even a Tesco Metro or a Sainsbury's Express. It wasn't an easy environment. It didn't look beautiful.

DP: When we met up with friends, it was always Stoke Newington Church Street, which has changed beyond recognition. Or the main Dalston drag: Centerprise, Ridley Road Market. We used to go shopping every Saturday, whether you wanted to or not, and it was just a hub of activity, it always had been. We used to frequent the second-hand shops, we dressed nicely, or what we thought was nice at the time. It had more of a community. This gentrification, I think it's lost everything, unfortunately. But

those are the places that we would hang out and meet and talk, go to clubs and stuff like that. Phebes, All Nations. It was vibrant, it had a real diverse community, people were into reggae, into ska, into lover's rock, you know.

TM: Hackney was not only diverse ethnically, particularly Kingsland High Street, Kingsland Road, Mare Street, Balls Pond Road – you would see somebody in a hijab or a burqa, you would see Roma people, you would see old Turkish guys – but it was also it was very diverse age-wise. That's something that I always feel very uncomfortable about when areas become gentrified: you suddenly lose your elderly and you lose young people, you don't see kids. But the thing is, about Centerprise or in the back streets, there were kids everywhere!

BB: Somebody in the group was clearly really into cars! Cos I know this sounds ridiculous, but nobody had a car. Nobody had the money to have a car. So that was a bit of wishful thinking there, going around taking photos of all the cars.

1984

Church congregation,
near the Rio

Waiting for the bus outside
the Pleasuretime amusement
arcades, Dalston Lane

MP Tony Benn, and protestors, at a march in central London *'Miners Solidarity Day – Coal Not Dole' newsreel*, 27 June 1984

The miners' strike

CT: The most important thing that came along was the pit strike. That changed everything in Hackney. Around here people felt like it was their last chance to, sort of, win against the Thatcher government.

BB: All the pits were being twinned with different parts of the country and Hackney was twinned with Oakdale.

CT: Miners from Oakdale and Nottinghamshire were billeted with MPs or Labour Party members. Glen was the central one of the Welsh lads, he stayed down here all the time, plus the four Notts blokes: Jed, Nobbie, Steve and Dave. They were crazy busy – that's how you made the money to keep the strike going. The NUM strike fund wasn't bottomless.

BB: The government saw it is a crunch moment and so did the miners, and so did everybody else… The miners could foresee that their livelihoods were going and what would happen to their communities. Because it wasn't like they all lived in different places, they literally lived around the pit. They knew that if the pit was destroyed, everything would be destroyed; and we knew that if the miners could be beaten, then anybody could be beaten. That was the purpose of standing up to the government's starving them back to work.

  We all felt powerless, and angry about being powerless. The miners were doing everything they could to challenge the situation and were being knocked back at every stage. Nothing was working and, meanwhile, the families' circumstances were increasingly dire…

It was probably one of the first times, I'd say, that there were food banks. People would collect food, donate food, try to raise money, there were loads and loads of fundraisers.

CT: We used to do collections every Saturday morning outside Dalston Sainsbury's. We got harassed by the police all the time, but people were just so generous – they didn't have much but they were prepared to give money to support something they knew mattered.

SH: The coming together of communities like Hackney and South Wales was incredibly potent… the resulting friendships and sharing experiences of such different lives was very meaningful for a lot of people, in both Oakdale and Hackney.

BB: We were always in with the protesters and we could get interviews and photos that maybe other people couldn't get, because it was quite clear the standpoint from which we were making these things.

On the box: OvenChips 15x2lb 01309 · FROM HACKNEY AFRICAN ORGANISATION 4 DALSTON LANE E8.

Hackney mayor Kenrick
Hanson passing over food to
be transported to South Wales
'Miners' Strike Hackney
to Oakdale food convoy'
newsreel, 1984

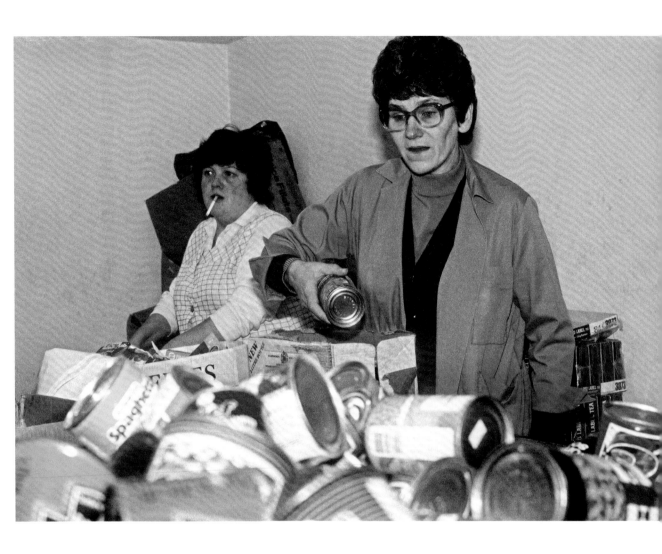

Hackney Council provided a
room in the Town Hall that was
used as a depot for the food
and other items collected in
the borough
'Collecting for Gwent miners'
newsreel, 19 December 1984

A colliery brass band on Stoke
Newington Church Street
'Gwent Miners in Hackney'
newsreel, 15 June 1984

Right
An RTSNG member at work
'TUC Day Of Action – Neasden 1'
newsreel, 11 February 1985

Below
A miner from Oakdale collects
for the strike fund. The RTSNG
recorded several incidents
where collectors were
threatened with arrest by the
police if they didn't move on.
Despite this, Hackney raised
a total of £110,000 during the
year-long strike
'Gwent Miners in Hackney'
newsreel, 15 June 1984

There were concerted efforts
across Britain by miners, trade
unionists and others to block
lorries delivering coal from
National Coal Board stockpiles
or imported from abroad –
thus causing blackouts and
disrupting the economy. This
is Neasden power station
*'TUC Day Of Action – Neasden 1'
newsreel, 11 February 1985*

1985

NEWS

ROUND UP

Right
Two years after the death of their son Colin, James and Pamela Roach (pictured, black coat, probably in 1983) were still demanding an inquiry into how he had died in the foyer of Stoke Newington police station

Page 158
Protest outside Stoke Newington police station on the second anniversary of Colin Roach's death, 12 January 1985

Page 159
The same night. These protests were always heavily policed and protesters were regularly abused, assaulted and arrested. Cat Thomas ('CT') is the blonde woman on the left

All photos from the 'Second Anniversary of Colin Roach's Death' newsreel, 12 January 1985

Independent Enquiry
ROACH FAMILY SUPPORT COMMITTEE

NO COVER UP

COLIN ROACH

The second anniversary of Colin Roach's death, 12 January 1985

CT: That particular evening we'd been doing the miners' collection in Dalston, and the chap who's wearing the blue bomber jacket came and said, it's the second anniversary of Colin Roach's death, we're going to do a demo outside the police station, do you want to come up. Everyone in Hackney knew about Colin Roach, so we said, yes, we will. And we did, mob-handed, because that's what people did. We all went on other protests, there was a certain solidarity with other campaigns.

BS: Trouble from the police? I don't remember ever getting into trouble except for at the Colin Roach demonstrations. I remember taking pictures of the police getting quite vexed and sort of... but we had fast legs and could get out quick.

CT: It was a slightly unpleasant shock to be settling down for an evening to watch a film – it must have been April, a few months later – and seeing a newsreel

of me shouting at the police! I was just relaxing and then there I was, on screen, three metres tall! It was unexpected because I wasn't directly involved in the campaign, I didn't know the family. If it'd been about the pit strike, I would sort of have expected to be there. That other woman? Never seen her before, I think she was just copying my look!

FH: It's just so, so clear, nothing has changed. You know, we're forty years older and nothing has changed, black men are still getting killed in police custody.

BS: I talk about Colin Roach and things that were happening, and try to explain to the kids that this has been happening from time, you know. We've always been protesting, and they think it's something new now – Black Lives Matter – and I'm saying to them, if you could just get together and unite like we used to, we'd get a lot more done.

The Hackney Book Bus

Hackney Library's Book Bus toured the borough's schools, playgroups and festivals, and imprinted itself into the memory of countless local children. The Book Bus followed a policy widespread in Hackney at the time of offering books free of the racist and sexist stereotypes foud in many children's books in those days

1985

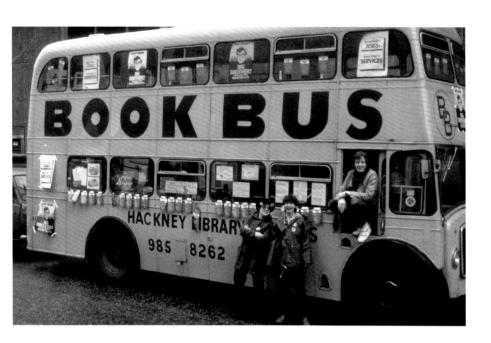

Below, left
Eddy Grant visits the Tekke
Music shop on Bradbury
Street. He played a gig at the
Rio in late 1982 or early 1983

Below, right
Musicians at Chats Palace

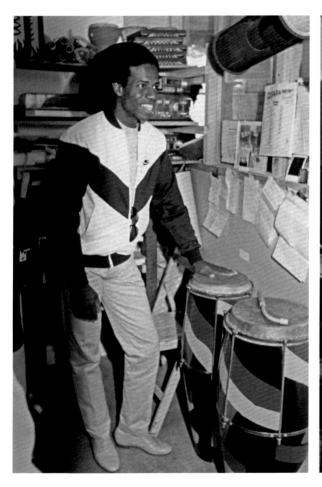

Music and dance

FP: That's what was so exciting about Hackney then, it was such a crossover. You also had a lot of South African musicians who ended up in Hackney because of apartheid, we had some really famous South African musicians living in Hackney at that point. There was Pyramids Arts, there was Four Corners, the film group Circles in Bethnal Green, run by a woman who ran a feminist film distribution. Lots of film collectives, you know, lots of grassroots art stuff going on.

EM: Most people had those ghetto blasters, you know, one person get a blast, everybody gather around, they listen to the latest records. And then at night, especially at weekends, there used to be sound systems, used to be parties, you'd pay to go in and a lot of people would... but then the police would come and raid it, or fights start, they kill each other, or something happen, you know. There was the Four Aces, yeah, and Phebes, they called it Trendz afterwards, it used to be owned by the Kray Twins.

I didn't go to every single club, but I went clubbing, and I went to the blues dances, the parties that finished at 6am. My sound system was Fatman. I followed Fatman, but Fatman was more in Tottenham than in Hackney. In Hackney it was Chicken. Chicken lived round the corner there. I used to go to Sir Tubby's, Fatman and Sir Doo's, cos I grew up in Islington. Coxsone? Yeah, Coxsone was more from south London, I think, but people used to go to Coxsone sound.

The police came to the point where they used to even lock up the sound system. They took the sound system to jail. Would you believe that? Police come and take all them big boxes and they take the food and go and eat in the station, the curry goat and rice.

Opposite
Formerly a 'super-cinema' and a circus, the Four Aces was a home for black music and was visited by Bob Marley, Stevie Wonder, Jimmy Cliff and Bob Dylan. Later, it became Labyrinth, a legendary acid house club, Two of the towers on Dalston Square, which replaced it, bear the name of Four Aces founders Newton Dunbar and Charlie Collins

Left and below
Occupying the former railway station entrance, Pleasuretime Amusements was a popular hangout. In the background, the auditorium of the former Gaumont cinema (AKA the Four Aces)

'Stoke Newington Festival'
newsreel, 1983

Breakdancing on the party
bus, Homerton Grove

Ridley Road Market

Jag Patel (co-owner, Party, Party):
Lots of things have happened on the street. *EastEnders* was made here. The producers came and sat upstairs in the warehouse studying the market for two years. They collected all the information they needed to come up with *EastEnders*. Quite a lot of the actors that initially were in *EastEnders* actually used to live around the corner. Each character was based on individual people that were in the market. Most of them are now gone.

KB: Somewhere like Dalston was a magnet for people, I think because Kingsland is a long road, and if you're arriving in a new area, what do you do all day? You walk up and down the road, and that's what a lot of people did. There was Ridley Road there, so you could get food cheap, and the area became a kind of thoroughfare for change, really, I suppose.

DP: Ridley Market, they used to sell clothes there. So, you'd go and find a nice jacket or whatever, barter around with the price.

And we had to go on a Saturday to get provisions, that was our main staple. You'd meet your friends, cousins, neighbours – 'How are you?' 'How are you!' – and then you'd get back on the bus and go home.

BB: All human life is represented down Ridley Road.

FP: Dalston was always such a wonderful place for food: Jewish cooking, Turkish cooking, West Indian cooking. And the bagel place on Ridley Road was always

such a treat. After gigs, all the musicians and the police were always there, at 3am. It used to be fun to talk to stallholders for interviews. Because the mindset was that you sold one product and you became the specialist in it. If you sold certain foods, people would come for that.

CT: The miners had a stall at Ridley Road Market at one point, during the summer of 1984. So there'd be all the fruit and veg, and the guys who worked there would be giving the miners fruit and stuff.

Page 168
The market seen from the first floor of Party Party, 9-11 Ridley Road (person unknown)

Page 169
Joyce Allen on her imitation flower stall; her sister Daphne Allen sold fresh flowers on Ridley Road, as did their mother Ada

Right
Violet Julian working on the Ridley Road egg stall

Opposite, below
Collecting signatures for a Stoke Newington and Hackney Defence Campaign petition demanding justice for Colin Roach. The leaflets read: 'Oppose Police Racism! Together we are strong!'

1985

Alan Cameron lying down on
the job on his fabric stall

Stallholder in a mask, possibly
for portrait project

AIDS

Maureen Carroll (later RTSNG member):
The AIDS newsreel we made, we put a huge amount into that. That became a standalone video which was, I think, sold on. So that was kind of a success – not only did it appear before the evening screening and the ads and whatever, but it also had another life. I don't know where it actually went, but it went places. AIDS was breaking out at that time, and people really didn't know, you know, where it came from. Was it the 'green monkey' disease? That's what they were saying. We were always

very careful: who knew if it really had started in Africa? We were very sensitive to all those potentially racist views that were around at the time, and we were trying to be sensitive to all marginalised groups, which was a huge feature of what the Tape/Slide Newsreel Group stood for.

Opposite
The office of the Terrence
Higgins Trust, which funded
and worked on the newsreel
with the Rio team. The
AIDS newsreel became a
widely used teaching tool by
organisations across the UK

Below
Slides from the AIDS newsreel,
and, below left, a response
from the RTSNG team to a
complaint about it

... and why they showed it

WE were interested to read Mr. C. Rees' letter concerning the AIDS newsreel recently shown at the Rio Cinema. As a group, one of the reasons for choosing AIDS as a subject for a newsreel was the sort of attitude expressed in Mr. Rees' letter towards (a) the "disease," and (b) homosexuality.

In general, media coverage of AIDS fails to inform people of the wider implications of the disease. Yes, some gay men have contracted AIDS, but one should not equate AIDS with being gay.

The AIDS virus lives in the blood and some body fluids, and though very few people actually contract the disease, potentially anyone coming into direct contact with infected blood can be susceptible. Gay men are just one group at risk; the disease can affect haemophiliacs, intravenous drug users, and those receiving blood transfusions.

We feel it is more important to find out all we can about AIDS, its implications for everyone and to feel compassion for those who are dying with it, than point accusatory fingers at the gay population. Homosexuality is a positive choice for many people and in this society it is made a very difficult one. Phrases like "fairy cake" are deeply and personally offensive, and shift the emphasis away from the very real problems of trying to contain and cure the disease. — DEIRDRE BLUNDELL, TONY BRENNAN, MAUREEN CARROL, ALLISON GREGORY, SANDRA HOOPER, FERN PRESANT, RIO CINEMA, KINGSLAND HIGH STREET.

Above and opposite
The first Terrence Higgins Trust
AIDS vigil in Trafalgar Square in
1985. Peter Tatchell is among
those lighting candles

Rate-capping

Part of the Tory project was capping the amount of money that councils could receive in rates – local taxes – which had the effect of forcing them to slash local services.

FH: The whole rate-capping thing brought Hackney to its knees. We needed to spend more money and we couldn't. We tried every which way, including many that were deemed illegal at the time, to protect our budget. There was the general air of private sector good/public sector bad, which of course has grown from there – but that was fundamentally when it started.

KB: More and more squeeze was being put on local councils, so they were able to do less and less in terms of services, and that had a knock-on effect. I ended up working for the council straight after [the Rio], in social services in one of the patch – area – offices. It was becoming dangerous simply because the people who would have had services in place didn't have services in place any more. They were so-called 'Care in the Community', but there was no 'care' element. It was just 'in the community', because that was cheaper. And so people would end up at Social Services offices because they had nowhere else to go. What do you do?

It became quite dangerous at times, more and more so. A social worker at our place was discovered to have a handgun in his top drawer. So, yeah, he was sacked.

DP: I remember one instance, we had an interview with Ken Livingstone and I was interviewing him about rate-capping, something like that and we forgot to turn on the microphone but he was very gracious. He said, 'Never mind, let's do it again.'

Opposite
Hilda Kean, leader of Hackney
Council, on the Town Hall steps
during the rate-capping crisis
*'Hackney Council –
Ratecapping' newsreel,
May 1985*

This page
Street protests and an
illustration of the effect of cuts
on Hackney council housing
*'Rate-Capping in Hackney'
newsreel, April 1985*

Right and opposite
The International Women's
Day celebration in Chesterfield
was organised by Women
Against Pit Closures; Oakdale
women attended the protest
*'International Womens Day
Chesterfield Rally' newsreel,
9 March 1985*

Below
A meeting of the Oakdale
Women's Support Group.
Josie (see text opposite)
is in the long red coat
*'Miners' strike – return to
work' newsreel, 1985*

The women of Oakdale and the miners' return to work

The RTSNG developed strong links with many of the miners' wives. And in 1985, when the government had crushed the miners, they were back in Oakdale.

BB: We did cover some of the men's stuff, but the men's stuff was being covered by other people, so we decided that we would work with the miners' wives – talk to them, take photos, and tell their side of things. The union very much was driving everything for the men, and the women were trying to get their families through

it, because a lot of the men were on the pickets the whole time.

MC: The most vivid experience for me was the day the strike was over. We went to the pit in Oakdale and we took photographs of the men going back down the mine to work, after a year on strike, having achieved nothing. We stayed with a woman called Josie whose husband had died from silicosis. She was really lovely; I had my little son Shane with me, who wasn't even one, and she minded him at her house while we took photographs at the pit. The women were singing the rallying songs they had been singing all through the strike. It was one of those moments in my life I will never forget.

CT: We all used to go to – the miners and the Support Committee and everyone – what is now the Rochester Castle, which was the Tanners' Hall at the time. It was the cheapest beer in Hackney, and miners are good at finding the cheapest pint anywhere! The pub had done good trade out of the Support Comittee being there all the time. We were in there when the strike failed eventually in March, all having a drink, and the miners started singing 'Solid as a Rock', which was the strike song. And the landlord came out and told us to shut up. We explained what happened and he said, 'I don't care, I'm glad you lost! I never supported you, and you're banned.' So I'm still banned from the Wetherspoon's. I've never been there since! Bastard.

It was a desolate time, really. I left Hackney for a couple of years after 1985, when the pit strike folded. I can still hardly bear to look at these pictures.

Opposite
Putting a brave face on it:
Oakdale miners and wives
at the pithead

Above
The miners strike ended
in defeat on 3 March 1985

Right
Miners' wives working at
Oakdale Comprehensive
School and Community College

*All from 'Miners' strike –
return to work' newsreel, 1985*

Hackney shops

From top row, left to right:
126 Lauriston Road; G. Moseley, Bradbury Street

T Hudson & Son, Stoke Newington Church
Street; Grodzinski, Clapton Common; Don's
Cafe Takeaway; Video, Stoke Newington Church
Street

Devote's Dalston Deli; Haro-Press Antiques,
Brooksby's Walk; Tokki, Bradbury Street;
Rainbow Co-op Bakery, Kingsland Road

185

Above
R. Mison, Wilton Way

Opposite, above
Mr Music, Kingsland
High Street (?)

Opposite, below
Mosquito Bikes workers'
cooperative, Bradbury Street

113
CHURCH
STREET

BITS + PIECES

Hackney sports

Opposite, left
Eastway Cycle Circuit was home to road racing in Hackney from 1975 until 2006, when it made way for the development of the London 2012 Olympic Park

Below
Clissold Baths

Other photos
After the match, Hackney Marshes

H A C K N E Y

1986—88

NEWS

ROUND UP

Albert Town / Butterfield Green

Albert Town was an area of south Stoke Newington, north-west of the Rio. It was bombed in the Second World War and by the mid 1970s many houses were in poor condition or derelict. Around 300 were demolished and, in 1986-87, the final phase of remodelling the area created what is now Butterfield Green around the existing adventure playground. In the photo opposite, top, the joists have been deliberately sawn through, probably by the council, to deter squatters

Hackney CND highlight the sale of UK lamb contaminated by radioactive fallout from the Chernobyl disaster, outside shops in the Angel, Islington. Many farms in northern England, Scotland and north Wales were affected; restrictions were not lifted for some UK farms until 2012

Both from 'Hackney CND in Islington' newsreel, 1986

Above
The Regent's Canal near the
lower end of Broadway Market

Opposite
Hoxton Market

Above
Hoxton Street Market

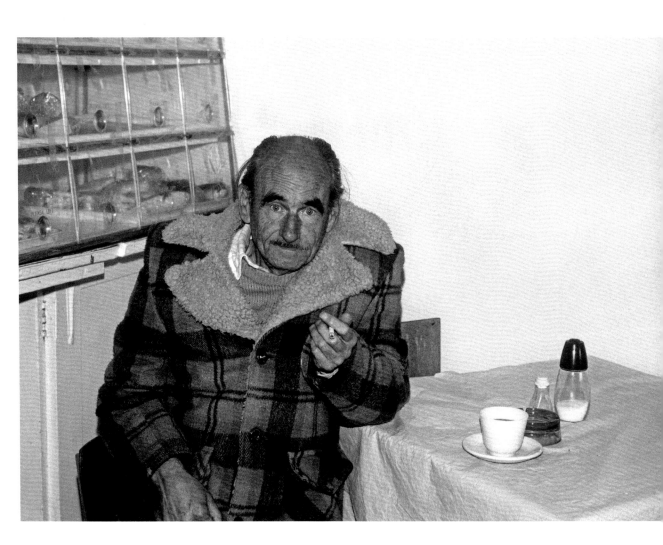

Columbia Road Flower Market

A fashion shoot for Bradbury Street's Tokki Boutique, with what is now Gillett Square and the auditorium of the Rio as a backdrop

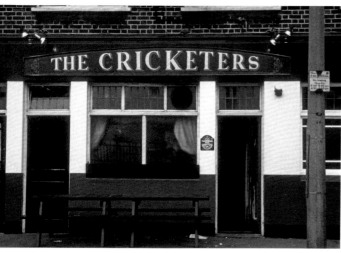

Hackney pubs

Opposite, from top row, left to right
The Anchor & Hope on the Lea at Harrington
Hill; Mr Pepys, Mare Street, demolished in 2000
to extend the Hackney Empire

The Cricketers, Northwold Road; The Goring
Arms, now The Dove, Broadway Market

Follies 'exotic' wine bar, formerly and currently
The Empress, Lauriston Road; The Mitford
Tavern, on the junction of Amhurst Road and
Sandringham Road, demolished in 2002

Above
Two members of the *Hackney Pensioners Press*

The Prince of Wales on
Lea Bridge Road, renamed
'The Princess...' in the 1990s in
honour of Princess Diana

The Sutton Arms, Boleyn Road

Travellers in Hackney

Throughout the 1980s there were several
Traveller sites in Hackney, whose occupants
were the target of prejudice and discrimination.
In this newsreel, 'Travellers in Hackney',
produced in November 1986, the man in
the trilby hat, pictured, is named as 'Mick
McCarthey, Official Spokesperson for the
Travelling People'

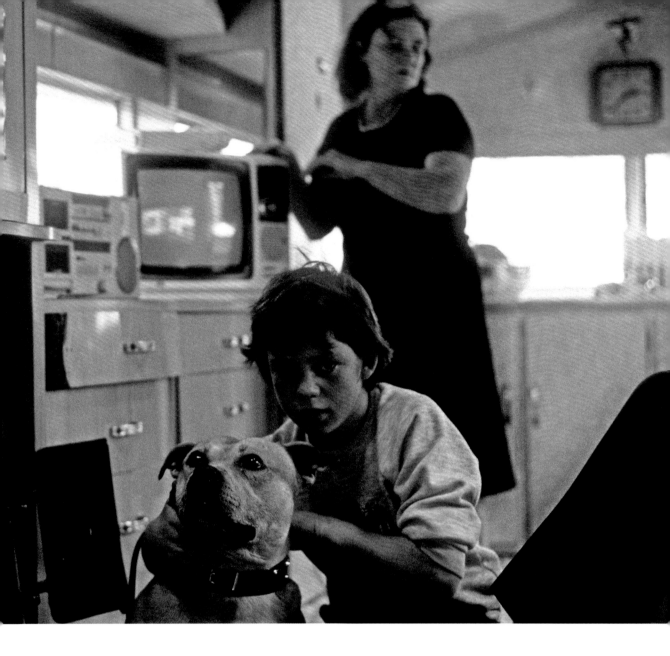

Opposite
Gransden Avenue

Opposite, below
Hackney Marshes

Right
'No Travellers served.
Strictly no dogs'

Below
Driving west under the
A12 on Wick Road

The Hackney Empire

The Hackney Empire, built as a music hall in 1901, was a Mecca Bingo from 1963-84. When in 1984 Mecca could not maintain its operations, blaming the rise of cinema and TV, Roland Muldoon of CAST spearheaded its reopening as a theatre for its 85th anniversary

All photos 1983, except, right: Roland Muldoon prepares to reopen the Empire on 9 December 1986
'Reopening Hackney Empire' newsreel, December 1986

Slide Ads

FH: The ads came in for a lot of criticism. They were considered by everybody, apart from the Rio staff, to be a complete pain. I felt they were really important because they put up local services alongside the main distributor of adverts. And they tried to refuse and not allow them – there was a whole standoff because the main distributor didn't want the slide ads to appear alongside whatever it was. They tried to stop us screening the slide adverts, which just seemed like a ridiculous David and Goliath sort of situation: 'We distribute to three-quarters of the world so you can't show ten slides advertising Indian restaurants.' It seemed to me to be one of the sillier fights I've had to fight.

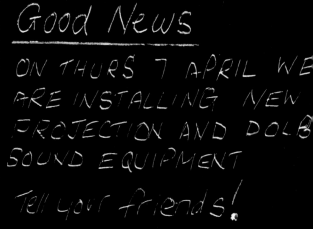

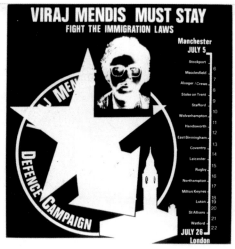

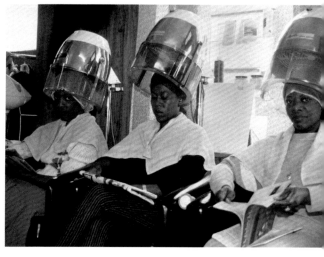

Hackney's favourite radical read!

*LOCAL NEWS *POLITICS
*GOSSIP *REVIEWS
*PUBS *WHAT'S ON

15p monthly.
On sale in the foyer.

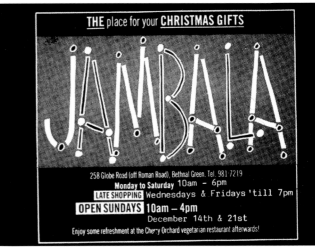

Squatting

Katherine Hornak (Hackney resident, pictured top right): Well, I was squatting then, in Cresset House by Well Street. I'd been there for about three-and-a-half years.
We had a little one-bedroom flat, me and my partner. There were quite a few squatters in the building, there were a lot of empty properties back then in Hackney.

Then the council decided, right, that's it, no more squatting. They started just evicting people, giving them really short notice to get out. But they kind of went past us – maybe they just didn't see us because the flat was so small, I don't know!

So we managed to stay quite a bit longer and I saw everything that was going on. What they were doing was evict the people and then just smash the place up. They smashed the toilets, sinks and stuff like that, so people couldn't move back in. And a lot of these flats had been done up really nicely. I mean, our little one, we never had any heating or hot water, because I could never get the boiler fixed, but I did have a gas heater in the front room and we got it looking really good. I was horrified, you know. There was a lot of homelessness at the time, that's why I got worked up. I actually don't remember ever going on any other protests, I think that might have been the only one!

A lot of the squatters from – was it Stamford Hill Estate? – they were up for a fight. We were a bit namby-pamby, I'm afraid, but I remember them coming over and giving us tips on what to do if the council turned up – you know, throw whatever at them – they really went for it! I actually don't know what the town hall meeting was about, could have been about housing. As soon as we all stormed in there, of course, they stopped talking. So I've no idea.

What happened was there was this big barricade of furniture, which we all clambered up to get onto the balcony, I don't know why we wanted to be up there. It was quite precarious and, if you look at the photo, they are helping that older fella up. My boyfriend is in the middle of the shot, my friend's at the top and I'm chatting away to another friend. The funny thing was, I had a family friend from Canada staying and we dragged him along as well. He's there, helping. He must have thought 'What's this crazy place!'

It seemed to go on forever! We were in there a good hour, could have been longer. I remember thinking 'I'm getting a bit fed up now.'

Then the riot police turned up, it got quite scary. Everybody was very good – we just left – but I can remember walking down these stairs, in a very confined space, with all the police lining up with their batons and shields and stuff, and I thought, if anybody kicks off now, this is going to horrendous. But we got out.

Opposite
Storming the town hall meeting, and evictions on the Stamford Hill Estate
'Stamford Hill Estate' newsreel, 1988

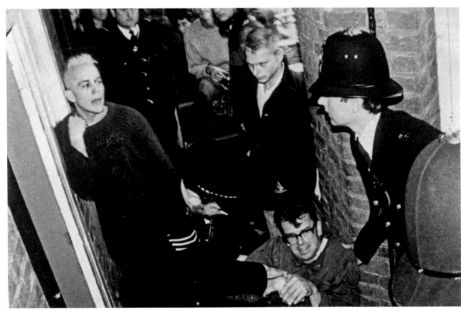

DP: It was nice going to people's squats, you knew people would be welcoming. It wasn't like 'What are you doing here?' it was 'Do you wanna stay for dinner?' It was really open, in stark contrast to what there is now, you know. People shutting the door: 'Get out! What you doing here?'

TM: We squatted a Victorian three-bedroom off Mare Street, and after two years we went to court to try and keep it. I'd personally fixed the roof, and we had rewired and replumbed it, it was lovely but freezing. We argued the council hadn't got any plans for it, so why were they issuing us with an IPO [interim possession order]? I wore the only suit I had – a blue linen one – and really enjoyed preparing for, and speaking in court! We lost, and moved out, but friends took over the house and stayed for another three years.

I remember back then there was something incredible like 7,000 empty properties in Hackney alone.

Opposite
Interviewing squatters
in Beatty Road

Right
Men in suits arrive at a squat
–possibly an eviction
'Stamford Hill Estate'
newsreel, 1988

Below
Outside a squat on
John Campbell Road

The Jewish community in Stamford Hill

For many years Stamford Hill in north Hackney has been home to Europe's largest community of Haredi Jews

Left
Yesodey Hatorah Girls' School

Below and opposite, top
Grodzinski on Clapton Common; in the 1960s Grodzinski was the largest kosher baker in Europe

Opposite, below
Playing on the River Lea
'One Day Off In Hackney'
newsreel, 1984

THIS RECORD — 'FIGHTING FOR SURVIVAL' —
THE SURVIVAL OUTFIT

CUTS

SURVIVAL

CELEBRITY AUCTION

SPIKE MILLIGAN

and DAVID

AUTOGRAPHED BOOKS AND ALBUMS BY

ELVIS COSTELLO   SCRITTI POLITTI   MELVYN BR

ARNOLD WESKER   GLENDA JACKSON

ROBBIE COLTRANE'S SWEATER.....

Spitting Image Stall   and lots, lots more.

Fighting for Survival

'Fighting for Survival' was a single by Survival Outfit – London hip-hop artists Daddy Speedo and MC Flyboy Dee – that supported the Save Hackney campaign.

KB: What we did, because it was a hip-hop record, was make the visuals fade as a photo came up. There was something in the mechanism that allowed you to fade in time with the scratching on the record without actually standing there doing it yourself.

It was part of a larger project called Jumbling for Survival! We had this great idea of having a 48-hour jumble sale on Ashwin Street. There was an empty factory which had been taken over by a local voluntary group. Clive who looked after it was a Rasta, and he was involved in Save Hackney somehow.

McDonald's and Ridley Road Bagel Bake, as it was then, donated breakfast. We got bands, a couple of them were quite well-known London bands, to perform, and there was an almost-all-night rave as well. Then community groups had jumbles, selling stuff during the day. It was bizarre, an absolutely mad idea.

We had a celebrity auction as well. Arnold Wesker, a local Hackney kid, signed a book and sent it down. Brian Clough sent a letter saying he couldn't attend because he had a match against Man Utd that day, but he sent down some Notts Forest stuff. And Robbie Coltrane gave us one of his gigantic-sized jumpers. I've still got the postcard upstairs that he sent to us saying, 'Yeah, you can have my Scottish TV jumpers. It's huge, come over on Sunday morning to pick it up.' He gave us the address and me and Lorraine turned up Sunday morning. He opened at the door and said, 'Nah!' He obviously thought that we were just people knocking to get his autograph. He took us in and gave us a drink, which was kind of him. I'd thought he was going to hit us!

Yeah, we had a load of weird stuff and the whole thing was opened by an actor called David Yip, who was a known TV star in the mid or late 1980s for something called *The Chinese Detective*.

No one made any money at all! But the *Hackney Gazette* was there, and a lot of people had quite a bit of fun watching the bands and doing bit selling, and at times it was completely packed

The 'Fighting for Survival' record was linked to that. Someone said, 'Oh we could do a charity record with it, as part of the auction.' So various people – not us – started getting the record together and asked around, and me and Lorraine used the tape/slide place to do the pictures, and put on the single at the Rio. I've still got the single somewhere, I've probably got the only copy left. Luddy Sams was involved as well. He was quite a well-known singer, with The Drifters and something to do with James Brown. He owned the Four Aces as well, which was not somewhere I ever frequented, but I remember it well! Friends of mine used to go down there, but I was too timid. That was in their skinhead days. That's all gone now, I think.

Broadwater Farm protest march

In 1985 an Afro-Caribbean woman, Cynthia Jarrett, died, having suffered heart failure during a spurious police search of her home on the Broadwater Farm Estate in Tottenham. Demonstrations over her death escalated into a riot, during which PC Keith Blakelock was violently killed. In March 1987, three local men were convicted of murder and sentenced to life imprisonment, despite no witnesses or forensic evidence. The Broadwater Farm Defence Campaign took up their cause and attempted to have the convictions overturned. In 1991 the 'Tottenham 3' were cleared, after evidence against them was shown to have been obtained under duress

One of several smallholdings
in Hackney in the 1980s, on
Richmond Road near the
junction with Mare Street

Left and below
Artist Adam Miller working with
kids at Hackney Downs School
*'Hackney Downs School Art
Project' newsreel, January
1987*

Opposite
Classroom, secondary school
unknown

Hackney housing estates

In the mid/late 1980s, the RTSNG covered some of the problems afflicting Hackney's housing estates, and attempts to address them, on estates like Buxton Court and in a borough-wide initiative, 'Hackney Estates – A Better Place for Women', which pledged £8 million to make estates safer.

AD: Up until the early 1980s, the Labour Party that ran the council were older, white, working-class men, basically. They lived on estates, they wore cloth caps, they'd been through the war. They had a strong identity. In the years after the war they saw their beloved borough fall apart: the work disappeared, their kids left home and then the place filled up with foreigners. And the young white people that turned up all had long hair and were taking drugs, you know, it was a sad time for them. But they were also quite powerful and they wanted to keep Hackney as it was in 1950, so housing policy, allocations of flats was racist: the nice, white working-class people with families would get allocated to small low-rise estates or street properties. Single parents, black people, people discharged from psychiatric hospitals, prisons, would end up in tower blocks on sink estates, there were lots of them.

EM: You had them rising up on the estates, like Pembury, for example. Estates where you'd find a large number of black and ethnic minorities, where the flats were in terrible condition, with mildew, and children were getting ill, asthma, all sorts of illness – and the council really wasn't good at repairing stuff. There wasn't many black and ethnic minorities working for

the council at the time, that's when they started an initiative to address it.

TM: A friend of mine worked in Hackney Council, and he was actually giving keys for cash. (Hand over about £1,000, jump to the front of the queue and get a flat.) He was part of the problem. He was so hilariously bent. God, you know, for council tenants, it wasn't funny. Friends in council flats had major problems that went unrepaired for years and friends in different boroughs would tease me that Hackney was this kind of Banana Republic... Hackney and Lambeth councils were kind of famous for being absolutely shit.

KB: My wife's parents were living in a council house in Paragon Road, and my mum was living in Clapton Park Estate. Clapton Park was okay, because it was relatively new, but Paragon Road, which was built in the late 1950s, the woodwork was falling to pieces and, you know, you could put job requests into the council but nothing ever got done. People ended up doing bodge jobs themselves, but some of it was quite dangerous – like, you had panes of glass that would start falling out in hot weather because they were puttied in. If it's four, five floors up and someone's walking down below, it's quite dangerous if a pane of glass is coming down through your neck, it'd be like a guillotine! ...

Buxton Court was the first big newsreel we did, about the problems on this small estate near City Road. They had major issues with damp in a lot of the houses and there were problems with window repairs. The council basically weren't fixing things and every time they came to fix something they didn't actually do a

A better deal for women

All from Hackney Estates –
'A Better Deal for Women'
newsreel, 1987

WOMEN, HOUSING AND VIOLENCE IN HACKNEY

Do you think the Council could make improvements to housing estates to increase security?

Early in 1985, the Women, Housing and Violence Working group of Hackney Council carried out a survey into Women's attitudes about security on estates.

This leaflet tells you more about the survey, but we would like to find out more about your views and experiences, to enable us to tell the Council about the sort of improvements that you want to see and make the right recommendations.

FREE POST Reply Card Inside

HOUSING SECURITY DESIGN GUIDE

Trowbridge Estate

The three 21-storey towers of the Trowbridge Estate in Hackney Wick were built between 1965 and 1969. Later, they were condemned as unfit for human habitation and – not without controversy and mishap – from 1985 onwards dynamited.

Both photos from 'Trowbridge Estate demolition' newsreel, 1987

good job, and things got worse and worse. There were a lot of health issues as a result of the damp that was in there.

We went round and interviewed a few of the families, and took pictures in their flats. Tried to talk to the council, but could never get any reply from them... That was the one I remember because we were going out and talking to people, meeting people. The sad thing was that the people who we were talking to said 'Which paper are you from?' We explained we weren't actually from a paper, and about the tape/slide newsreels at the Rio, and eventually, once they understood, they said, 'Yeah,

that's fine, advertise it in any way, shape or form. Maybe something will come of it.' There was no one really fighting their corner, and, in a sense, you can understand why the press weren't picking it up, because I don't know how many properties under Hackney Council's remit were in a mess in those days.

Carole Jasilek (later RTSNG member): We were up on one of the 'streets in the sky' and I remember us walking along taking photos till we kind of got to the corner, a blind corner, somebody could have been hiding there. That bit I really remember.

The estates were really run down, that was the whole idea behind the £8 million [government funding]. There were lots of boarded-up windows, boarded-up doors, lots of graffiti, rubbish, stray dogs wandering around. I don't remember gangs hanging around or anything like that, but they were run down. Things like lifts not working, going up the dark, dank stairways... but then pockets where the estates looked better kept, and quite a few elderly residents, if I remember. Not much greenery, a lot of concrete. We took photos of the nicer parts as well – which I think was an idea the councillor

had – photos of front gardens and more greenery and flowers, and pictures of where they were doing bits up, putting up better lighting.

We had a dilemma, I recall, as to who was going to have the final say in the newsreel: whether we were going to go with the councillor who was really positive, like, 'We've got £8 million and we're going to do this, this and this,' or the resident who was saying, 'Well, they talk and they talk but nothing gets done.' In the end we decided to go with the resident because that was throwing a bit of a gauntlet down to the council.

Buxton Court

Opposite
Buxton Court under repair

This page
Hackney Environmental Action Resource (HEAR) was engaged to survey Buxton Court. Their report revealed broken and exposed asbestos panels, and problems caused by condensation and damp, including black mould, sodden carpets and wallpaper, and rotten windows. Tenants demanded the removal of asbestos from all homes, ventilation for bathrooms and toilets, double glazing and central heating. Improvements came slowly

All photos from 'Buxton Court' newsreel, September 1987

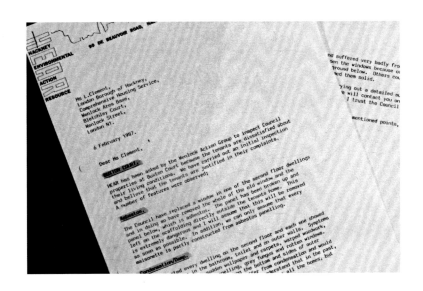

Regeneration

As the 1980s wore on, with squatters evicted, some council housing improved and many derelict properties bought for renovation, the area began to change.

BS: People moved in and they started taking... I had quite a lot of friends that were anarchists and they were very angry at the yuppies, as we called them, moving in, taking over the housing. We couldn't get any housing! But what happened is the houses looked better, the area came up, it was more presentable, had more character to it, it looked more respected.

When you think about it now, being more mature, you think 'God, it was a fucking dump!' But at the time I didn't think Hackney was a dump because I'd grown up here. You just think 'Life is hard, I can't get a job, I can't get anywhere to live.' When you're squatting, you don't think 'Oh, I wish I was like the Joneses,' you just get on with it.

SH: There was quite movement of people getting squats recognised and money

being made available for housing co-ops. The Everbrook Housing Co-op came up at that time. I think the way they started was that they were able to let out properties as short-life housing while funds were found to develop them and make them into permanent housing. I was only involved at the short-life level stage.

BB: Stoke Newington has always been the most gentrified part of Hackney, and Dalston always had a sort of cool cachet to it, but I don't think anyone could have predicted exactly how gentrified it would all become. At the time nobody could have imagined that any house, anywhere, would be worth a million pounds! It's a different world.

Opposite
Council houses in Seal Street under renovation

Above
As well as private renovations, cooperatives such as Everbrook were restoring housing in Hackney

The Dalston Cycle Path Campaign

In 1987 the RTSNG reported on the Dalston Cycle Path Campaign, which proposed turning the recently closed railway line from Dalston Junction to Broad Street Station into a safe cycle and pedestrian route into the City

All from the 'Dalston Cycle Path Campaign' newsreel, December 1987

Green Hackney

Right
Mayor Kenrick Hanson awards
the LS Davis trophy at the
Hackney Housing Estates
Gardeners' Society annual
Flower and Vegetable Show
at the Town Hall

Below
The serious business
of judging the entries

Opposite
Hackney allotments

The Great Storm

The famously un-forecast storm on the night
of 15/16 October 1987 caused damage across
the UK. In Hackney, 100mph winds sent high-
rise residents from the Nightingale Estate in
Lower Clapton to seek shelter in the police
station because one of the (since demolished)
tower blocks was swaying, and fifty families
from Northwold Road were evacuated after
an uprooted tree caused a gas leak. More than
2,620 trees are estimated to have been brought
down in Hackney alone

*All photos from 'Stoke Newington Hurricane
Winds' newsreel, 1987*

HACKNEY

Endings

NEWS

ROUND UP

The end of the Tape/Slide Newsreel Group

Keeping the newsreel group running became increasingly difficult. Details are unclear, but for a time it appeared to become women-only and somehow interwoven with the Women's Media Resource Project that was also housed in the basement.

It eventually disbanded sometime in 1988. Some of the big later projects – including a major newsreel on Wendy Savage, the women's reproductive rights pioneer – are lost. However, for many members the tape/slides had a lasting impact.

RC: As Thatcherism permeated local government and society, the levels of subsidy started to decline. I'm sure that was a serious consideration in how the Rio evolved from then on. Equally there was a decline in community organisations and perhaps a general sense of declining community identity as the gentrification of Hackney started to take hold.

SH: Those friendships [made at the RTSNG] became so strong. I think it was in part due to our engagement with politics, very physically in terms of going and getting involved in the miners' strike, being on the lines outside the police station… something happens to people when they become so committed to something, it's different on social media.

DP: Greenham Common and the miners' strike, they made me more politically aware. Actually being involved – putting a face to people's lives and experiences – changed the way I approached my adulthood, the things that I put my time towards. So, yes, it made quite a difference.

CJ: Doing the project gave me a lot. When I went down to London I had totally lost all my confidence… the project, and being in Hackney, basically changed it all around for me. And I never looked back after that.

CSL: Being a teacher in Hackney and learning to teach photography in that way was a real education. I'm very proud of what I was taught, actually, by my colleagues and the young people.

WK: My experience with the newsreel team made me very open to being involved in community media. Within three months of arriving in Australia, I started volunteering for an inner-city community radio station. In some ways it was a bit like a radio version of the slide newsreel… The people I got to know through working there led me, either directly or indirectly, to almost everything that has happened in my life since, including a stint of reasonably well-paid work in Afghanistan, in 2006-7, as technical adviser and project manager for an organisation that built and maintained community radio stations there. Through a rather twisting path, I have the Rio Tape/Slide Newsreel Group to thank for that experience!

BB: People understood that it was a group for unemployed people, so if you got a job, you had to leave. In my case I went to college *and* got a job – I was so delighted to get a job at the Rio!

KB: While I was doing my job at the Rio, I was also working for Hackney Council part time, as a schools' finance advisor. That came about as a result of my involvement

with the Tape/Slide group and the voluntary work I was doing: they were the levers I was able to use at the council, and at the Rio as well... A lot of people used their voluntary-sector experience to get jobs afterwards. Because otherwise you had no experience and there was still a lot of unemployment at the time. It was a fairly major issue.

SH: I think some people who came to the Rio avoided watching the newsreels, maybe went to buy their ice creams. Because, you know, it was a very low-tech experience for people who were probably coming to watch a big-screen movie. But it

had its core of people committed to it and we covered some really significant issues.

KB: It was dark, so you could never really gauge people's reactions, but some people must have taken notice! I don't think it changed the lives of too many people watching it, but does any piece of journalism do that?

CT: You always had a sense, then and still, I'd say, that the Rio belonged to us locals. And being shown things that happened locally was quite important. It made us feel that we mattered.

Two of the intrepid animators
limber up for the Rio's
Saturday morning kids club

The view towards the City
from the Rio roof

Acknowledgements and thanks

Thank you to all of the people at the Rio and those connected to the RTSNG who have helped us with our research and given interviews.

First of all, that means all the participants listed on page 15 at the front of the book – this could not have been done without your willingness to think back a long time to what was for many a difficult period, and to share your recollections. These oral histories have added to making this book an important document of Hackney in the 1980s.

Thanks especially to Eveline Marius for her poem 'Down in the Ghetto' (p 68) and for her poetry accompanying 'One Day Off in Hackney' (p 132), both used with permission. And also to Ngoma Bishop for helping identify people in some of the pictures.

Thank you to Zawe Ashton and Michael Rosen for their Forewords, Zawe's written while moving house and Michael's while recovering from Covid-19.

Then also thank you to the following people for sharing your knowledge of Hackney people, places and events, or for helping us in some way in our work: Susan Baldwin, Ray Blackburn, Anna Brueton, Rebeka Cohen, Mick Coward and Steve Crook, Simon Denney, Laurie Elks, Christine Jackson, Fiona Johnston, Hilda Kean, Sarah Mudd, Jenny Mules, Selina Robertson and Anne Robinson, Charles Rubinstein, Rosa Schling, Che Singh, Nicola Stephenson, Maureen Taylor, David Walters, Winstan Whitter and Ken Worpole.

Dr Benjamin Zephaniah's recollections on page 47 are taken from the *4WardEverUK* article 'Zephaniah Remembers Colin Roach', used with permission under a Creative Commons licence and with no changes. Links here: http://bit.ly/4wardZephaniah and https://creativecommons.org/licenses/by/4.0.

An extract of his poem 'Who Killed Colin Roach?' (same page) is used with Dr Zephaniah's permission. Thank you.

CLR James's speech, an excerpt of which appears on page 48, was recorded in *Celebrating C.L.R. James in Hackney, London* (edited by Gaverne Bennett and Christian Høgsbjerg, Redwords, 2015). The interview with Mackenzie Frank, quoted on the facing page, was conducted in 2015 and appears in the same book. Mackenzie Frank worked as a community librarian for Hackney Council for seven years from 1983, and helped organise the CLR James week of activities in 1985 around the renaming of Dalston Library.

Thank you to Julia Bard and the *Morning Star* for permission to quote from her article 'Old, Female and Up for the Fight' (p 60), readable in full here: bit.ly/morningstarhpp

The words of Jag Patel, co-owner of Party, Party (p 168), are taken from *Ridley Road Market* (Tamara Stoll, self-published, 2019) and are used with permission.

Thanks more generally to the team at the Rio: Oliver, Yoan, Tim, Alex, Marisa, Dorsa and Denis.

Finally a huge thanks to the Kickstarter supporters and to the thousands of followers of the @riocinemaarchive Instagram account – for your love, enthusiasm, comments and detective work identifying the people and places in the archive images posted there.

Keep spreading the love.

Rio Tape/Slide Newsreel Group members

These are the names, taken from Rio lists, annual reports and other sources, of members of the Tape/Slide Newsreel Group. The list is probably not exhaustive, or even correct, as records (and spellings) were erratic. The authors of this book attempted to contact everyone but could not find, or did not receive a reply from, some. To those we did not speak to, we hope you enjoy the book.

Paul Bellini; Deirdre Blundell; Keith Braid; Lorraine Braid; Henry Bran; Tony Brennan; Sally Bull; Maureen Carroll; Patricia Coates; Sandra Greaves; Susan Hallidane; Carole Jasilek; Will Kemp; Debbie Kershaw; Kenneth Laing; Linda Lassman; Zita Lomax; Stella Lymas; Eveline Marius; Maxine (?); Antony McGrane; Sean McGrane; Thembi Mutch; Dee Phillips; Fern Prasent; Helen Saunders; Barbara Schulz; David Skerritt; Felicity Stephen; Diane Willmott.

In addition to these names, more than fifty members of the public also contributed photographs to the 'One Day in…' and 'One Day Off in Hackney' newsreels.

0°04'31"W

51°32'58"N

If you recognise yourself or others in these photographs, please let us know, via Hackneyinthe80s.com or the @riocinemaarchive Instagram

Cover photos

Front
Friends, Kingsland High Street
'One Day Off in Hackney' newsreel, 1984

'THE END'

Hands off the NHS
'St Leonard's Hospital Protest & Occupation' newsreel, 6 July 1984

Back
'GLC Anti-Racism Festival' newsreel, 6 July 1984

Working at the Hoxton Trust

Christmas shopping at Ridley Road Market
'One Day in Hackney' newsreel, 13 December 1983

First published in October 2020
by Isola Press, London
IsolaPress.com

Forewords and essays are © the respective named authors. Except where indicated in the acknowledgements, interviews were conducted by Alan Denney, Max Leonard, Tamara Stoll and Andrew Woodyatt. Their editing and arrangement in this book is © these authors.
All photos © the Rio Cinema Archive
This selection of photos © Isola Press.
The moral right of the authors has been asserted.

Design: Myfanwy Vernon-Hunt
This-side.co.uk

Typeset in Lettera Text

Printed and bound by Gomer Press, UK
Gomer.co.uk

Printed on GardaPat 13 Kiara
and Colorit Chamois

ISBN: 978-0-9954886-6-3